Cambridge Elements

Elements in Public and Nonprofit Administration
edited by
Robert Christensen
Brigham Young University
Jaclyn Piatak
University of North Carolina at Charlotte
Rosemary O'Leary
University of Kansas

BUREAUCRATIC RESISTANCE IN TIMES OF DEMOCRATIC BACKSLIDING

João V. Guedes-Neto
Brazilian School of Public and Business Administration at FGV

B. Guy Peters
University of Pittsburgh

Shaftesbury Road, Cambridge CB2 8EA, United Kingdom

One Liberty Plaza, 20th Floor, New York, NY 10006, USA

477 Williamstown Road, Port Melbourne, VIC 3207, Australia

314–321, 3rd Floor, Plot 3, Splendor Forum, Jasola District Centre, New Delhi – 110025, India

103 Penang Road, #05–06/07, Visioncrest Commercial, Singapore 238467

Cambridge University Press is part of Cambridge University Press & Assessment, a department of the University of Cambridge.

We share the University's mission to contribute to society through the pursuit of education, learning and research at the highest international levels of excellence.

www.cambridge.org
Information on this title: www.cambridge.org/9781009548182

DOI: 10.1017/9781009437479

© João V. Guedes-Neto and B. Guy Peters 2025

This publication is in copyright. Subject to statutory exception and to the provisions of relevant collective licensing agreements, no reproduction of any part may take place without the written permission of Cambridge University Press & Assessment.

When citing this work, please include a reference to the DOI 10.1017/9781009437479

First published 2025

A catalogue record for this publication is available from the British Library

ISBN 978-1-009-54818-2 Hardback
ISBN 978-1-009-43746-2 Paperback
ISSN 2515-4303 (online)
ISSN 2515-429X (print)

Cambridge University Press & Assessment has no responsibility for the persistence or accuracy of URLs for external or third-party internet websites referred to in this publication and does not guarantee that any content on such websites is, or will remain, accurate or appropriate.

For EU product safety concerns, contact us at Calle de José Abascal, 56, 1°, 28003 Madrid, Spain, or email eugpsr@cambridge.org

Bureaucratic Resistance in Times of Democratic Backsliding

Elements in Public and Nonprofit Administration

DOI: 10.1017/9781009437479
First published online: September 2025

João V. Guedes-Neto
Brazilian School of Public and Business Administration at FGV

B. Guy Peters
University of Pittsburgh

Author for correspondence: João V. Guedes-Neto, joao.neto@fgv.br

Abstract: This Element investigates how public employees react to illiberal policies proposed by authoritarian leaders during democratic backsliding. Using survey experiments employed with 942 bureaucrats from the United States, the United Kingdom, and Brazil, the research explores their willingness to resist the implementation of illiberal policies. Findings show a significant readiness for resistance. The results indicate varying levels of resistance across countries, with Brazilian bureaucrats showing the highest, followed by British and American counterparts. Additionally, within-country analysis identifies individual characteristics affecting the intent to resist. The Element explores the dynamic relationship between politicians and bureaucrats, the autonomy of civil servants, and the perils of working under autocratic leadership. It also underscores the need for tailored strategies in recruiting and retaining public employees to uphold democratic values. These findings shed light on the complex dynamics between bureaucrats and democratic governance, emphasizing the importance of safeguarding institutions in times of authoritarian challenges.

Keywords: democratic backsliding, bureaucratic resistance, politics of bureaucracy, survey experiments, comparative public administration

© João V. Guedes-Neto and B. Guy Peters 2025

ISBNs: 9781009548182 (HB), 9781009437462 (PB), 9781009437479 (OC)
ISSNs: 2515-4303 (online), 2515-429X (print)

Contents

1 Introduction   1

2 A Theory of Bureaucratic Resistance   7

3 Bureaucrats and Politicians in Three Selected Countries   20

4 Empirical Tests   25

5 Findings   34

6 Discussion   46

   References   54

1 Introduction

The illiberal era in politics has had consequences not only for the politicians involved, and for the citizens of the affected countries. It also has had significant consequences for the public bureaucracy. The public bureaucracy in most democratic countries is assumed to operate under some form of public service bargain (Hood and Lodge 2006) in which they provide neutral competence in the advice rendered to ministers and in the implementation of policy in exchange for anonymity, permanence, and influence. While there may be variations in the details of that bargain (see Staranova and Knox 2024) the basics are similar across countries but are now being challenged in a number of settings.

The bargain between principals (politicians) and agents (civil servants) is based on an assumption that both sides of the bargain are principled, and are operating within broad normative standards defined by constitutions and political traditions existing within government (Bertelli 2021). Specifically, these traditions include the acceptance of minority rights, basic political rights for all citizens, and the rule of law. Unfortunately, the illiberal period has been characterized by "unprincipled principals" who have often ignored the usual rules governing their behavior (Brierley 2020; Schuster et al. 2021; Schuster, Meyer-Sahling, and Mikkelsen 2020). In particular, they have sought to reduce the autonomy of the civil service and to make it more politically attuned (Morelli and Sasso 2020). For example, one of Donald Trump's last acts as president in his first term was the creation of the Schedule F appointment, an excepted service form of recruitment for public employment without traditional civil service protections like job stability – in fact, this new provision could result in reclassifying thousands of career employees, multiplying the number of political appointees in the federal government (Moynihan 2022). He is persisting with similar actions in his second term and has revived Schedule F (Wagner 2025).

In addition, these political leaders have not felt themselves constrained by the values of liberal democracy (see Yesilkagit et al. 2024). They have attempted to aggrandize their powers (Bermeo 2016) and, to do so, attacked and persecuted those bureaucrats who did not comply with their expectations (Lotta, Tavares, and Story 2024; Moynihan and Roberts 2021; Sá e Silva 2020; Story, Lotta, and Tavares 2023). Many of these illiberal leaders, such as Viktor Orbán in Hungary, the Law and Justice Party in Poland, López Obrador in Mexico, Donald Trump in the United States, and Jair Bolsonaro in Brazil have undermined aspects of the rule of law and sought to limit the civil liberties of citizens, especially immigrants and minorities (Bauer et al. 2021). These leaders have also engaged in attacks on the institutionalized civil service and sought to politicize the public bureaucracy.

Even political leaders who are not as extreme as some of the illiberal leaders have begun to move away from some of the values and practices usually associated with liberal democracy toward favoring a more politicized and majoritarian form of governing. Electoral outcomes, rather than laws and constitutions, have become a sacred value in many political systems (Peters and Pierre 2023). Thus, in many contemporary governments civil servants face the possibility of being given orders by their superiors that are illegal, or essentially political rather than governmental. In many cases, they are illiberal, attempting to undermine democratic norms other than simple majority rule. The conventional remedies available to civil servants in coping with political pressures may not always work with more committed leaders, and the public servants may have to consider more extreme alternatives (Schuster et al. 2021). The "guardrails" that have been constructed over decades to protect the civil service have been questioned, and in some cases swept away by, illiberal, populist leaders.

It is therefore important for students of public administration and policy to come to grips with these changes in the relationships between civil servants and politicians, and to consider the impacts that increased attempts at political control are having on the civil service as an institution, as well as on individual public servants. While these efforts at controlling the bureaucracy to some extent come and go depending upon the particular politicians and political parties that may be in office, there does appear to be a general trend toward attempts to impose increased political controls over the civil service.

The concern with the attempts of illiberal political leaders to impose their controls over all of government, including the bureaucracy reverses the long-standing concern of public administration theory with democratic controls (and political controls in a more authoritarian regime). Going back to Max Weber, the concern had been the danger of *Beamtenherrschaft*, or bureaucratic domination. Contemporary political leaders refer to this domination as the "Deep State" or the "Administrative State," and assume that it exists, and want to find ways to replace it with a simple, majoritarian political domination (Fukuyama 2024; for an alternative perspective see Waldo 1948).

This Element will address the difficult situation faced by many contemporary civil servants, and perhaps one that will be faced by more as populist parties appear to be making headway in countries such as the Netherlands, Italy, France, India, Argentina, and the Philippines.[1] This is an important challenge not only for individual civil servants but also for their governments and their

---

[1] There are some differences between illiberal and populist; however, given the common ground between both adjectives in current politics, we often use the terms interchangeably.

citizens. We will be discussing the threats to the traditional bargains in terms of the autonomy of the public bureaucracy, and the fundamental issue of the legal accountability of government. How much autonomy should individual bureaucrats, and their organizations, have from political control, and what options should be available to them to combat what they consider to be excessive control?

Although we will focus on the decisions of individual civil servants, the same type of questions can arise at an organizational or institutional level. If an illiberal political leader seeks to undermine the policies of an agency, and does so through suspect means, are the civil servants justified in acting in concert to protect their programs and their clients? If not, are they complicit with the forces that seek to undermine the programs and the laws that created them (Bozeman et al. forthcoming)? In some cases, civil servants may seek collective responses to resist the actions of the political institutions of government. For example, French civil servants were considering large-scale protests had a government of the far right come into power in the 2024 election (Trippenbach 2024). In other cases and perhaps more commonly, as we will show, resistance occurs through individual action, including different means, such as shirking and sabotage (Brehm and Gates 1999). One example is the practice of whistleblowing (Hollibaugh Jr., Miles, and Newswander 2020).

The central question in this Element is *"Are bureaucrats willing to use their power to resist the undemocratic policies of illiberal leaders?"* We will focus on illiberal governments, but the same questions can apply to more conventional political leaders as well. Indeed, the question for the more conventional leaders may be of even greater concern. A politician who does not have the personalistic and bombastic style associated with illiberal leaders may be able to push their civil servants in ways that the more obvious illiberal leaders could not. The politicization literature, for example, has discussed "functional politicization" (Hustedt and Salomonsen 2014) in which pressures are applied to make career public servants perform their tasks in line with the wishes of their political leaders, and even take on political tasks in addition to their governmental tasks.

The autonomy and control issue in public bureaucracies has both empirical and normative dimensions. There is a good deal of research that documents that civil servants, especially senior civil servants, are able to exercise substantial autonomy in different political systems (Bersch and Fukuyama 2023; Carpenter 2002; Huber and Shipan 2002; Yesilkagit and van Thiel 2008). Even within fully democratic regimes that degree of autonomy will vary across time. For example, various American presidents have claimed the existence of a "unitary executive" in which the bureaucracy should have no autonomy but is merely an extension of presidential power (Driesen 2020). President Trump has institutionalized this type of system with his "Schedule F" and other measures that have undermined the autonomy of the civil service. Given the magnitude of the tasks of contemporary governments, such a centralized position appears infeasible, and bureaucrats continue to exercise some autonomous decision-making. Illiberal leaders, then, pursue different channels to curb autonomy. Some will distribute political appointments to their loyalists, going beyond traditional modes of patronage that are focused on partisan alignments (Panizza, Peters, and Ramos Larraburu 2023). For example, Jair Bolsonaro appointed a considerable number of former military personnel to high and mid-level positions, as a manner of assuring compliance with his requests. In some cases, they adopted abusive practices to force compliance among career bureaucrats (Story, Lotta, and Tavares 2023).

The normative question about the autonomy of civil servants is more difficult, given that it is to some extent culturally embedded, and linked to administrative traditions (Peters 2021). The Wilsonian tradition in the United States, appears to provide little room for autonomous action by civil servants, while bureaucrats in Napoleonic systems appear to have much greater latitude for action, always within the bounds of law. Even with that cultural variance, however, there tend to be some common expectations about democratic governance derived from political theory and from law. In particular, there are some common standards of liberal democracy and its relationship with bureaucracy that have been generally accepted (Heath 2020), and these have been in general the targets of illiberal leaders who want, or demand, more personal and majoritarian styles of governing.

From the existing literature in public administration, we know that civil servants will not necessarily obey their superiors' orders in every circumstance. Brehm and Gates (1999) discussed the famous triad of *work, shirk,* and *sabotage* as possible reactions to desirable and undesirable expectations. It is true that, more often than not, bureaucrats will prefer to do some work rather than none (Pierre and Peters 2017), and tend to have a professional commitment to their jobs in the public sector (Liou and Nyhan 1994; Mendez and Avellaneda 2023; Suzuki and Hur 2020). Still, there are cases when the principal-agent bargain will be disrupted. Rosemary O'Leary (2019) describes it as a *guerrilla government* when public employees will actively work against their superiors. More recently, this has been illustrated by several cases of whistleblowing (Hollibaugh Jr., Miles, and Newswander 2020), among other types of guerrilla response (Bersch and Lotta 2023). Further, there are an increasing number of instances in which civil servants openly oppose the actions of the government by street demonstrations, and so on (Khan et al. 2024).

There are different reasons for breaking the bargain. Gailmard and Patty (2007) suggest the "slacker and zealots" alternatives. Using part of Downs' (1965) terminology, *conservers* will likely resist whenever new policy directives are about to bring change, while *advocates* may decide on how to act depending on the policy's impacts on their organization. While civil servants may have different motives for breaking the bargain, from the perspective of the general observer, there is a normative preference for the neutral, Weberian bureaucrat to comply with the expectations of their superiors, provided that they are presented within the legal framework.

Most of the discussion of shirking and sabotage has been negative, as implied by the very terms used to describe the actions, However, there can be cases in which, as mentioned earlier, the civil servants are policy advocates or even policy entrepreneurs (Bourgault 2011). This policy advocacy may be for substantive policy change, or it may be more reflexive, attempting the preserve or enhance the working conditions of public servants, as well as to enhance their roles in governing. For example, civil servants during the National Performance Review in the United States were major participants in attempts to alter the role of the civil service (Peters and Savoie 1994).

There are cases, however, when such expectations will be different. What if implementing a certain policy means reducing the individual rights of the population? What if this means eroding democracy? In these cases, the general observer operating with a democratic normative foundation may well have an ethical preference for a disruption of the traditional principal-agent bargain. The question, then, is whether civil servants are willing to resist if tasked with the implementation of such policies.

There is evidence that sometimes civil servants have a difficult time resisting political pressures, especially when an illiberal regime is in power for an extended period of time. Philippe Schmitter (1971) interviewed senior-level bureaucrats during the military dictatorship in Brazil to find that many of them had been coopted by the regime. Cooptation occurs because of the fear of losing their status quo, their job, or even their life. In Venezuela, during the Chavez-Maduro regime, many bureaucrats were sidelined or even persecuted for opposing the government's ideas (Muno and Briceño 2021). This is similar to the Exit, Voice, and Loyalty triad (see Hirschman 1970). Even in less extreme cases, civil servants may decide that they can do more good for the society inside the government than outside. There are cases when exit and voice are simply too costly, and loyalty – whether genuine or feigned – becomes the only viable alternative for them.

Despite these challenges, we argue in this Element that there are cases when voice becomes the dominant strategy. We chose three cases for our study: Brazil under Jair Bolsonaro, the United States under Donald Trump, and the United Kingdom under Boris Johnson. While these cases differ significantly in various aspects – such as state capacity, administrative traditions, and bureaucratic protections – they offer valuable comparisons.

Hansen and Sigman (2021) developed a State Capacity Index that measures factors like administrative efficiency and bureaucratic quality, ranging from –3 (lowest state capacity) to 3 (highest). In 2015, Brazil scored 0.738, while the United Kingdom and the United States scored 1.777 and 1.860, respectively. However, the pattern reverses when considering bureaucratic closedness, a concept introduced by Dahlström, Lapuente, and Teorell (2012). In this regard, Brazil's civil service ranks as the second most protected in the world, trailing only India. Meanwhile, the United Kingdom and the United States share similar scores, both falling below the median in a ranking of fifty-two countries.

Furthermore, at least Boris Johnson was not necessarily an illiberal populist – or, at least not to the degree that Bolsonaro and Trump were (but see Alexandre-Collier 2022; Lacatus and Meibauer 2022). In line with this argument, the literature provides robust evidence of Bolsonaro's (e.g., Lotta, Tavares, and Story 2024; Story, Lotta, and Tavares 2023) and Trump's (e.g., Guedes-Neto 2024; Moynihan 2022; Moynihan and Roberts 2021) attacks against the public service. Boris Johnson engaged in actions against his country's civil service less often and more subtly (see Rawnsley 2020), focusing most of his incendiary rhetoric against "Brussels bureaucrats" (S. E. Hanson and Kopstein 2022). Yet, bureaucrats of the three countries faced important challenges, in many cases facing policies that went against their values and, sometimes, democratic norms. In Section 3, we further explore the differences and similarities of these three cases to propose that our empirical findings are likely to be generalizable across most of the democratic world.

In those three countries, we surveyed convenience samples of bureaucrats in all levels of government. We were interested in their willingness to resist when assigned to implement an undemocratic policy. Acknowledging that resistance could be perceived as a sensitive topic, we employed different experimental techniques to isolate social desirability bias. To begin, our questionnaires included two list experiments that causally estimate the proportion of respondents willing to resist. We further employed a vignette experiment to isolate whether the intent to resist took place due to the counter-democratic nature of the policy or simply because bureaucrats disliked the policy they were supposed to implement.

We also must be careful not to assume that civil servants would actually resist just because they said so in an experiment. There are no costs associated with complying with the democratic norms in the survey, but there may well be in real life. Our tests attempt to assess this issue, but we recognize that attitudes will not necessarily equate to behaviors. We added some robustness checks that address this issue at least partially. Section 4 includes these and a series of additional tests to causally estimate willingness to shirk and sabotage in Brazil, the United States, and the United Kingdom.

The good news is that most of the respondents were willing to resist. Our empirical evidence remains robust to different experimental tests, inferring strong causality to our claims. The bad news is that part of this willingness to resist occurs because bureaucrats simply dislike a given policy (regardless of whether this is democratic or not). This *resistance dilemma*, as we further discuss in the following sections, is key to understanding democratic backsliding processes, as well as to discussing the issue of autonomy in public administration.

Section 2 of this Element will develop the theoretical perspective concerning bureaucratic autonomy more fully, and will discuss autonomy, especially in the face of democratic backsliding. That theoretical discussion will be followed by an empirical analysis of the willingness of civil servants in three countries to engage in what might be seen as extreme forms of autonomy when faced with extreme decisions by politicians. This analysis will stress the conditions under which the civil servants will be most willing to engage in these activities in the three countries. We will return to the fundamental issues of autonomy in the conclusion, discussing how our empirical findings relate to the normative and theoretical foundations.

2 A Theory of Bureaucratic Resistance

Our concern with the role of the public bureaucracy in contemporary politics and policymaking leads us to consider how the bureaucracy may counter what may be considered illiberal pressures by contemporary politicians, and protect the established rule of law within democratic regimes. At the extreme, the bureaucracy may adopt the role of "guardian" (Yesilkagit et al. 2024) to protect the constitutional order against a more simple-minded majoritarian conception of democracy (see Peters and Pierre 2022).

As we consider this emerging role for the public bureaucracy, several strands of literature help to inform and provide a foundation for this role for the bureaucracy. The first of these, and the primary focus of the inquiry, is the pursuit of autonomy by the bureaucracy, and related attempts of politicians to control the powers granted to the bureaucracy. The pursuit of bureaucratic autonomy is also related to the literature on the relationship between politicians and bureaucrats that provides various conceptualizations of the roles that both sets of actors play in the governance process. The literature discussing the relationships between actors can also be related to the now large literature on the politicization of the bureaucracy (Staranova and Knox 2024).

2.1 Bureaucratic Autonomy

Finding an appropriate balance between accountability and autonomy is a major underlying question in public administration. On the one hand, holding civil servants, accountable for their actions is a central value in governance, especially democratic governance (Bovens, Goodin, and Schillemans 2014; Finer 1936). Ministers are supposed to hold their civil servants accountable, and then the legislature enforces accountability over the ministers. Even though accountability has become more complex and multifaceted (Olsen 2017) this more traditional form of accountability remains an important component of democratic governance.

On the other hand, however, the civil service is supposed to enjoy some autonomy and to be able to exercise independent judgment as it applies laws, and provides policy advice to the government (Lynn and Robichau 2013). The civil servants are expected to be experts in their tasks, and to employ that expertise to make the best possible decisions, and provide the "frank and fearless" advice that political leaders need. While civil servants are meant to serve their political leaders, they are also responsible for law and ethics, and are expected, again in the conventional description of democratic political systems, to act separately from political leaders (Friedrich 1935).

Beyond legal compliance, bureaucrats are also driven by their personal convictions and institutional loyalties. While Weber (1947) championed a formalistic impersonality – *sine ira et studio* (without hatred or passion) – it is well established that civil servants, like all individuals, hold personal preferences that inevitably shape their decision-making (Peters 2018). These decisions may be influenced by self-interest, organizational priorities (Downs 1965, 1967), or even a commitment to safeguarding the state from undemocratic forces (Yesilkagit et al. 2024). Ultimately, the extent of bureaucratic autonomy and an individual's willingness to exercise it determine how civil servants navigate their relationships with elected officials.

Although the autonomy of civil servants has been discussed most frequently concerning upper-level civil servants, it is also important for street-level bureaucrats who make decisions about clients, and who are engaged with local communities in adjusting policy (Nabatchi and Amsler 2014). Political leaders appear to be more concerned with whether senior civil servants will agree with them than with what actually happens when lower-level officials implement the programs.

The conflict between accountability and autonomy for civil servants has been central in public administration theory, and has been enshrined in the writings of Max Weber (1978) and Woodrow Wilson (1887), as well as numerous scholars coming after them. While both foundational scholars emphasized the importance of accountability, they also recognized the need for civil servants to be able to make their own decisions as they apply the law, and therefore to be free of political interference. The underlying logic was that, while implementing the law, civil servants should be able to make their own decisions and then be held accountable (Sager and Rosser 2009). Civil servants were assumed to be professionalized, with values and service commitments defined by their profession, and therefore could be trusted to make the right decisions in most instances.

This conflict of autonomy and accountability also appears in the familiar debate between Carl Friedrich (1935) and Herman Finer (1936) over accountability, albeit phrased in terms of forms of accountability (see Heidelberg 2020). Friedrich (1935) argued that the inner controls of civil servants, and their adherence to the law, were sufficient for accountability, and further that politicians were often poorly equipped to influence administrative decisions. This conception of the roles and capacities of civil servants would put them in a central position in governing, with political leaders legitimately having limited direct control over the decisions made by civil servants. This internalized version of accountability gives civil servants great autonomy. It can also put them in conflict with their nominal superiors in public organizations who can claim greater legitimacy because of their connection to the electoral process.

Herman Finer (1936), on the other hand, argued for more control from politicians, and more direct responsiveness of administrators to their political supervisors. In this view, the civil servant should do what he or she is told, and be willing to be over-ruled if they make a decision that does not conform to the wishes of the minister or other political leader. Thus, very little autonomy of action is acceptable, and the civil servant is directly accountable for actions. Consequently, in this view, the civil servant has little latitude for independent judgment about performing their tasks. It also implies some degree of politicization of the civil service, as they are expected to be highly responsive to their political superiors, rather than to their own professional values. When one encounters illiberal political leaders this view of accountability can also put them in the position of having to decide whether to accept illegal or immoral orders.

Phrased differently, Friedrich (1935) was willing to accept more autonomy for civil servants, while Finer (1936) wanted more control and more direct intervention by politicians, or perhaps by the courts and other oversight bodies, to enforce accountability. Both components of this dichotomy of accountability and autonomy must be considered carefully as viable options for organizing government. On the one hand, it is important that policies are shaped by elected officials, and that the rest of government accepts the electoral mandate. On the other hand, however, civil servants are professionals and experts, so they should be empowered to make decisions within their sphere of competence.

To further explore bureaucratic autonomy, consider Bersch and Fukuyama's (2023, 214) definition as

> the ability of executive agencies to use their own discretionary authority to implement policies made by political principals, as well as to make policy according to their own wishes when mandates are ambiguous, incomplete, corrupt, or contrary to their perception of national interest.

The definition includes at least five elements that merit discussion in the context of bureaucratic resistance. They are (1) the agents, that is, executive agencies, (2) discretionary authority, (3) ambiguity and incompleteness, (4) corruption, and (5) national interest.

Framing organizations as the agents of resistance implies unified thinking or, in other words, a consolidated organizational culture. Each agency will hold its specific interests and act to protect them. To illustrate, the U.S. Environmental Protection Agency (EPA) will likely use its powers to deter environmental crimes regardless of the presidential administration's partisan leaning. Ozymy, Menard, and Jarrell (2021) find that the EPA has been capable of sustaining the stability of its criminal prosecutions over time despite the expectations of different presidents. This includes periods when the administration was clearly hostile toward the agency, for instance, those of Ronald Reagan and Donald Trump.

The Bersch and Fukuyama definition also makes the decisions made by civil servants to be unconstrained except for those five criteria, and to follow their "wishes." While the delegation of authority to executive agencies does provide latitude, these decisions cannot be "arbitrary and capricious," to use the language of the Administrative Procedures Act in the United States. Rather, those decisions must be in compliance with the public employee's attributions, adequate technical standards, and the rule of law.

We posit that organizations are not the exclusive agents of decision-making. Despite organizational pressures, individuals hold their own values and may have significant discretion to affect policy implementation. Coyne and Hall (2018), for instance, describe how public employees acted as policy entrepreneurs to push for relevant decisions impacting the current surveillance policy in the United States. In another study, Brazilian civil servants used their discretion, technical expertise, and political motivations to play a key role in the implementation of transportation policy and a river's cleanup (Guedes-Neto 2022). Also, the street-level bureaucracy literature is filled with examples of individuals exercising their own discretion while implementing policy (Hupe 2015). In all examples, autonomous bureaucrats were not necessarily acting on behalf of their agencies, nor following the expectations of elected officials.

Discretionary authority, as mentioned before, creates a pathway for bureaucratic autonomy. Elected officials do not possess the time or knowledge to fully control the policy process, especially compared to the structural role and expertise of public employees (Downs 1967; Huber and Shipan 2002). Politicians, therefore, delegate decisions to the bureaucracy, whose actions are likely to be influenced by a series of factors – politicians' expectations being only one of them. After all, as Carpenter (2002) demonstrates, elected officials often know that going against the values of specific agencies may be inefficient and politically costly. One example regards the confrontations between the EPA and hostile presidential administrations. Prior research finds that bureaucrats relied on "hidden actions" within their legal possibilities to sustain their agenda (Ozymy, Menard, and Jarrell 2021), for instance, transferring resources from one action to another (Ringquist 1995) and using their statutory authority to set fines (Auer 2008).

Incomplete or ambiguous policies may be easy targets for bureaucratic decision-making (Baier, March, and Saetren 1986). Again, it does not necessarily mean that they were poorly designed. It is possible that they are purposefully ambiguous to allow public employees to make decisions depending on the nature of times or, as Downs (1967) posits, based on their considerably higher expertise in such areas. These cases need not represent instances of bureaucratic resistance, since even Herman Finer would likely agree that some degree of autonomy is essential for policy implementation. Still, they facilitate resistance if bureaucrats decide to use them to go against the interests of elected officials.

Corruption and national interest are often both catalysts and focal points of bureaucratic resistance. Consider corruption first. When politicians exert significant control over public employees' careers, they can more easily co-opt bureaucrats to facilitate rent extraction from the state (Brierley 2020). This dynamic helps explain why Dahlström, Lapuente, and Teorell (2012) find that countries with stronger meritocratic recruitment systems tend to experience lower levels of corruption.

While bureaucratic autonomy can enable officials to misuse their discretion for personal gain (Nieto-Morales, Peeters, and Lotta 2024), it also provides them with the independence needed to resist corrupt practices without fear of retaliation (Dahlstrom, Lapuente, and Teorell 2012; Meyer-Sahling, Mikkelsen, and

Schuster 2018). Empirical evidence suggests that, more often than not, corruption is driven by heightened political control rather than by bureaucratic autonomy.

The protection of the national interest follows a similar logic. Formally, elected officials have the legitimate power to design and implement policies on behalf of the population. Still, they may use this legitimacy to benefit cronies rather than the general public (Haber 2013). Worse, they may aggrandize their own powers, therefore weakening the democratic system and produce democratic backsliding (Bermeo 2016).

In one of his seminal articles, O'Donnell (1994) argued that one of the perils of the third wave of democratization was that some of the newly minted regimes stagnated at the "delegative democracy" stage. This meant that elected officials had substantive powers to govern without any accountability throughout their terms. In such cases, it is hard to claim that electoral mandates are sufficient to assure that public officials are governing based on the national interest when they are not held accountable by checks and balances.

In these cases, public employees may use their discretion (statutory or not) to influence policy outcomes. As proposed by Yesilkagit et al. (2024, 415), they should follow "a conception of the state that is not neutral in the classic liberal sense, but protective of liberal principles of governance." The challenge here is that one should expect that bureaucrats would hold values more closely associated with the national interest (in this case, the liberal democracy) than those held by politicians – an assumption often dismissed by, among others, Public Choice scholars (Tullock 2005; Tullock, Seldon, and Brady 2002). We, thus, echo Yesilkagit et al.'s (2024) proposition that we must strengthen what they call state guardianship that function as additional checks and balances against illiberal politicians.

2.2 Bureaucratic Politics

In considering the autonomy of the civil service, we should remember that civil servants, and government organizations, are not necessarily passive actors waiting for the rules to be defined by others (Dahlström and Lapuente 2022; Peters 2018). Rather, they may be interested in carving out some greater scope for independent action (Downs 1965; Gailmard and Patty 2007; Guedes-Neto 2023). Whether done overtly or by stealth, there is a continuing political struggle within government, a form of bureaucratic politics, that attempts to clarify the rules of the game for accountability, autonomy, and policymaking (see Bach and Wegrich 2020; Peters 1987).

The autonomy of bureaucracy, and of individual public servants, is one of the classic questions in the comparative study of public administration. This is generally not phrased in terms of autonomy per se but more often in terms of the extent to which political leaders are interested in, and capable of, controlling the public service. The other way in which this question can be seen is in the extent to which public servants attempt to pursue a policy agenda of their own, as opposed to being willing to accept the directions of their political leaders (Aberbach, Putnam, and Rockman 1981).

The political conflict between politicians and civil servants can be seen through a number of lenses. One has been the traditional lens provided by Max Weber (1978) and Woodrow Wilson (Wilson 1887). Others have sought to develop a taxonomy of the types of interactions (Peters 1987). Others have conceptualized the relationship between these actors as a bargain, with public servants ceding direct control over policy in exchange for less overt influence over policy, as well as permanent appointments (Hood and Lodge 2006). Still, others have examined the capacity of public servants to act as policy entrepreneurs and to be a more active participant in the policy process (Coyne and Hall 2018; Silveira, Cohen, and Lotta 2024; Zhang, Zhao, and Dong 2021).

While this literature on politicians and bureaucrats began with the ideas of Weber and Wilson, it has evolved to accept that public servants have, and indeed should have, a good deal more autonomy from the control of politicians. Some of this shift has reflected the ideas of "empowering" public servants to make more of their own decisions (Peters and Pierre 2000) as a means of improving the morale and performance of these public employees. In addition, there has been a greater understanding of the importance of allowing civil servants to make more decisions simply because they have more information, especially about applying law to individual cases at the street level.[2]

The study of politicization of the bureaucracy has been the logical extension of the study of relationships between politicians and their public servants. Political leaders rather naturally want their civil servants not to be autonomous, but rather to be committed to their same goals as the government of the day. Therefore, whether by attempting to control who becomes or remains a public servant, or by exerting control over their behaviors while in office, there have been attempts to control bureaucracy (Neuhold 2014; Peters and Pierre 2004).

2.3 The Illiberal Era and Bureaucratic Autonomy

This debate about the autonomy of public servants has become more significant during a period of democratic backsliding and increasing politicization of the

---

[2] Most of the literature on the relationship between politicians and bureaucrats is focused on the higher levels of the civil service who are involved in designing policies. The same questions need to be asked, however, about the lower echelons of public organizations who are in direct contact with the public.

bureaucracy. As illiberal political leaders assume office, questions of the autonomy of bureaucrats to make their own decisions are crucial for the quality of governance and democracy (Bauer et al. 2021; Lotta, Tavares, and Story 2024; Moynihan 2022; Moynihan and Roberts 2021; Peters and Pierre 2019; Story, Lotta, and Tavares 2023). Given that the policies favored by these illiberal leaders have frequently been questionable legally, and may violate fundamental civil liberties, individual civil servants may have to make their own decisions about whether to exercise some autonomy or to accept directions from the new political leaders.

The attempts to politicize the bureaucracy have become extremely intense and, in some cases, successful, in the illiberal era. For example, Victor Orbán in Hungary has gained a very high level of control over the bureaucracy there (Hajnal and Boda 2021), and the Law and Justice Party had in Poland until defeated in the election of 2023. During his first term in power, Donald Trump attempted to politicize the American bureaucracy by dismissing all members who did not agree with his policies, and has promised to extend his control if he is reelected (Moynihan 2022; Moynihan and Roberts 2021). In fact, when Trump returned to the presidency in 2025, many of his first executive orders demonstrated his willingness to fulfill his promise.

An autonomous and capable bureaucracy appears to threaten the agendas of illiberal leaders – and those leaders seem to be recognizing that. On February 7th, 2025, The Washington Post detailed how federal bureaucrats were resisting Trump's orders (Davies 2025). In the article, Jocelyn Samuels, a former commissioner at the Equal Employment Opportunity Commission (EEOC), stated, "If I wasn't going to use my position to speak out for what I think is right as a matter of law and policy, I might as well not occupy the position at all." On January 28th, *Government Executive* reported that she had been fired (Newhouse 2025).

The question of the autonomy of civil servants to make decisions under illiberal regimes leads to two familiar trichotomies. The first is Albert Hirschman's (1970) idea of exit, voice, and loyalty. Does the civil servant who does not agree with current policies leave the government, does he or she complain about the policies, or do they merely remain and do their job? There is some evidence of civil servants leaving the government under leaders such as Donald Trump (Guedes-Neto 2022; Moynihan and Roberts 2021), Jair Bolsonaro (Sá e Silva 2020), and Viktor Orbán (Hajnal and Boda 2021), but most have chosen to remain.

For those who choose to remain in the civil service during an illiberal regime, there is yet another trichotomy of choices about how they will perform their duties: working, shirking, and sabotaging (Brehm and Gates 1999). Civil servants can choose to *work* as they have throughout their careers (faithfully following directives from their superiors), they can choose to *shirk* their duties and do as little as possible for programs with which they disagree, or they can attempt to *sabotage* the regime's programs (Schuster et al. 2021). The latter two choices involve the civil servant trying to evade accountability to elected officials, and pursuing their own conceptions of what constitutes appropriate government action.

Both shirking and sabotage can be seen as a form of voice in Hirschman's trichotomy. One involves the civil servant displaying discontent with the regime by minimizing his or her contribution to the mission of the agency.[3] Sabotage is a more extreme behavior, involving undermining in some way the performance of the organization and the delivery of a program in which the civil servant does not believe. That lack of support may come from a policy disagreement, or in the illiberal era it may arise because the civil servant believes the policy undermine basic constitutional principles (Yesilkagit et al. 2024).

2.4 Bureaucratic Resistance

The willingness of public servants to resist commands from their political superiors and to pursue goals that they deem more appropriate has been discussed several ways in the public administration literature Rosemary O'Leary (2019) has discussed this behavior as a "guerilla government" and Jan Olsson (2016) has described it as "institutional subversion." At an organizational level, this resistance to controls can be considered as a search for organizational autonomy and the pursuit of organizational goals (perhaps mandated by law or democratic norms) rather than accepting instructions from politicians. Further, career civil servants may believe that they better represent those organizational goals, and perhaps even the goals of government as a whole, than do the short-term inhabitants of ministerial positions.

Resistance may occur for different reasons and through different channels. Hollibaugh Jr., Miles, and Newswander (2020) fielded a conjoint experiment with American bureaucrats to demonstrate that policy disagreements, ethical concerns, and the policy's negative impact influence their willingness to disobey their principal or engage in confrontation, delay compliance, or whistle-blow.

In addition to this, the literature shows that some bureaucrats will actively mobilize support from external actors (Milhorance 2022; Milhorance et al. 2024; Waisbich 2024), such as nonprofits and international organizations, to safeguard their policy priorities or, at least, to avoid policy dismantling. While these studies focused on bureaucratic resistance during the illiberal administration of Jair

---

[3] There is an argument that shirking among bureaucrats is more common, and does not depend on the nature of the regime in power. However, there is relatively little evidence to support that generally negative conception of the civil servant (see Pierre and Peters 2017).

Bolsonaro in Brazil, there is also evidence that public employees will mobilize external actors to advance their policy preferences in normal times, even when these may not be aligned with the priorities of elected officials (Abers 2019; Abers and Tatagiba 2015; Rich 2013).

As an example, consider Donald Trump's executive order "Restoring Accountability to Policy-Influencing Positions within the Federal Workforce" (January 20th, 2025). On his first day in office for the second term, the president explicitly wrote that "In recent years, however, there have been numerous and well-documented cases of career Federal employees resisting and undermining the policies and directives of their executive leadership." The executive order, then, acknowledged the existence of bureaucratic resistance and aimed at recreating the Schedule F career (see Moynihan 2022), which grants the presidency increased powers to hire and fire at will. Other presidential acts followed the same trend. That is, for Trump, the issue was relevant enough to merit such responses.

We build our analysis of the possible types of resistance of bureaucrats on the study of Brehm and Gates (1999) and their trichotomy of "working, shirking, and sabotage." The logic of this analytic scheme is that most civil servants will perform their assigned tasks most of the time (Pierre and Peters 2017). However, when confronted with negative working situations they can either shirk, or do as little as possible, or actually sabotage the work of the organization.[4] These latter two options, and especially sabotage, involve their violating the usual terms of their employment, and therefore represent significant career choices for them.

We agree with Perry and Wise (1990) that, in general, public employees will hold a "public service motivation." This means that they opted-in for the public administration due to their willingness to serve the population. We assume that, at least in democratic contexts, this means that civil servants will attempt to preserve their public organizations as much as possible based on the perception that they provide a desirable service to the population. In this sense, new leaders attempting to impose an illiberal policy would be going against their interests and the interests of the population they serve. Therefore,

> H_1: *On average, civil servants become more willing to resist when assigned to implement undemocratic policies compared to other policies.*

---

[4] In terms of Hirschman's (1970) familiar trichotomy of "exit, voice and loyalty" both shirking and sabotage may be seen as forms of voice, with one obviously a more extreme version than the other. Brehm and Gates (1999) refer to a fourth reaction – neglect (see Withey and Cooper 1989). Yet, in the context of bureaucratic resistance, we treat shirking and sabotage as types of voice.

The willingness of civil servants to resist commands from their political superiors may be a function of several personal and organizational factors – including, but not limited to, their democratic values and policy preferences. We, however, opt for discussing a less obvious variable. Consider perceived job status. Resistance comes at a cost. We have previously mentioned the case of Jocelyn Samuels, the EEOC commissioner fired by Trump. In some cases, illiberal leaders will remove their opponents from the public administration. In other cases, when job stability is more protected, illiberal politicians and their allies will engage on abusive supervision (Story, Lotta, and Tavares 2023), sidelining (Muno and Briceño 2021), or even political persecution (Hajnal and Boda 2021). It is natural that before resisting, public employees will calculate the costs of their actions.

When civil servants believe that they could easily find a well-paying job in the private sector, the fear of being fired does not represent a high cost – at least not as high if compared to those who believe they could not find a good job in the private sector. To corroborate, Selden and Moynihan (2000) find that bureaucrats are less likely to quit the higher their salary is. In such cases, the risk of becoming unemployed would likely demotivate some civil servants to defy their bosses' preferences.

Llorens and Stazyk (2011) argue that public–private salary equity is not a strong predictor of turnover. Even if that is the case, the perception of better opportunities should still matter for decisions to shirk or sabotage. Those who do not perceive the difference between public and private salaries as important may have opted to work for the government in the first instance not due to income but because of their public sector motivation (Perry 2000; Perry and Wise 1990) and the ability to help society. To a certain extent, this resembles what de Graaf (2011) calls the "by-the-book professionals." The label regards those public employees who are not loyal to the stakeholders of their organization, but to society and its citizens. In his own words, "blindly following the minister is not something a professional [of this kind] should do" (de Graaf 2011, 295).

Following these two rationales, we hypothesize that:

H_2: *Those civil servants who believe that they would be (financially) better off in the private sector will be more likely to resist undemocratic policies.*

Our next proposition follows from the previous. Fear of punishment for shirking or sabotage should be the starkest among those who do not enjoy job stability (Tullock 2005). While the rational choice approach may justify this proposition based on the employees' self-interest of preserving their jobs, there is also the issue of political control. Cornell and Lapuente (2014) propose that in meritocratic administrations, where most civil servants enjoy job stability, democracy tends to be more stable given the constraints imposed on political action (see also Cornell and Grimes 2015) taken by superiors to punish subordinates.

This argument is at the root of Wilson's proposition of separating politics and administration. In fact, he concludes his seminal work with a series of questions, one of them being:

> How shall our series of governments within governments be so administered that it shall always be to the interest of the public officer to serve, not his superior alone but the community also, with the best efforts of his talents and the soberest service of his conscience? (Wilson 1887, 221)

This summarizes his proposition that a merit-based administration, insulated from politics, should not serve solely at the will of a political superior, but also in response to the public interest and its own conscience. If, however, the spoils system prevails, public officers must obey their superior's orders alone to preserve their employment.

To be sure, the merit system does not eliminate the politics from the bureaucracy. Civil servants have their own preferences, motivations, and agendas. However, by assuring meritocratic recruitment and retention, bureaucrats need not to align their politics with the politics of their superiors. This allows tenured bureaucrats to disobey elected officials when faced with illiberal expectations. Of course, this also comes with the cost that resistance may occur even when elected officials attempt to implement policies that are not illiberal.

Even though the merit system has become the norm in most democratic countries, not all public employees are tenured. Some enter the government through political appointments, others are hired through temporary contracts, and so on. Nontenured employees will surely face higher costs of resistance than tenured bureaucrats. This should influence their decision to resist illiberal orders. Thus, we expect that tenure operates as a constraint against political control over the bureaucracy since it grants career bureaucrats more autonomy to resist illiberal policies with fewer risks of facing punishment than untenured public employees would.[5]

We hypothesize that:

> H_3: *Tenured bureaucrats should be more willing to resist than untenured public employees.*

Finally, we hypothesize that one factor affecting resistance by bureaucrats is whether the individuals themselves are supervisors. The closer a public

---

[5] This can also be related to the arguments of Dahlstrom and Lapuente (2012) about the relative desirability of closed administrative systems.

employee is to the principal (in this case the political leader), the harder it is for him or her to resist. Tullock (2005) argues that bureaucrats interested in career advancement will opt for following the orders of their superiors. Aberbach and Rockman (1995) find support for this proposition at least among public employees who become loyalists to new administrations regardless of their individual preferences.

While supervisors may enjoy more formal autonomy in directing their teams, their positions are often contingent upon maintaining alignment with political leaders. If they resist political directives or fail to adequately implement political priorities, they face removal from leadership roles. This dynamic creates a powerful incentive for compliance, despite their nominal autonomy. The need to secure their position within the bureaucracy often outweighs their ability to act independently. As a result, supervisors may be less willing to resist undemocratic policies compared to lower-level bureaucrats, who are further removed from direct political oversight. This reinforces the argument that proximity to political actors can constrain resistance, even among those with greater managerial discretion.

This leads to our last hypothesis:

H_4: *Supervisors are less likely to resist undemocratic policies than subordinates.*

This proposition is also close to another ideal type of top manager proposed by de Graaf (2011): the "society's neutral servants." They are the "most loyal to their ministers and have the fewest conflicts with them" (de Graaf 2011, 296). These managers do so not necessarily act in this manner because of possible personal gains, but because they believe they are serving society when following orders. Not all supervisors will indeed be like that, as pointed out earlier (see de Graaf 2011). However, we propose that the higher someone is in the hierarchy, the closer they will be to political actors and more willing to take direction from those politicians, whether for the sake of greater benefits or their willingness to implement the orders of their principals.

We should remember, however, that those in the upper echelons of the bureaucracy will be more experienced and more knowledgeable about policy, and therefore may be more likely to have ideas of their own. The reactions of highly placed bureaucrats therefore may be substantive disagreements with their ministers, or with political advisors. The job of the civil servant, in addition to following the directions of their political superiors, is to provide "frank and fearless" advice – something they cannot do if they only tell their superiors what they want to hear.

2.5 Summary

This section has discussed two trichotomies that can describe the behaviors of civil servants when confronted with policy decisions with which they do not agree taken by their political leaders. While the majority of civil servants will be loyal to their organizations and do their work as expected, there are situations in which some will seek to leave the organization or will not work as diligently as they might normally. In the extreme, there are times in which some civil servants may decide to attempt to undermine the work of the organization, especially when they receive orders that they consider illegal or immoral. The likelihood that civil servants will engage in shirking is, we argue, increased by illiberal leaders who seek to undermine liberal democratic values.

This section has developed a series of hypotheses about the behavior of civil servants when faced with leadership within their organizations that may be advancing illiberal proposals. Although much of the bureaucratic autonomy literature emphasizes the organizational basis of autonomy, we are focusing our research on the individual level, and the hypotheses assess the extent to which the characteristics of individual civil servants may affect their behavior vis-à-vis illiberal political leadership. This is an enduring question in public bureaucracies, but has become especially relevant with the growth of populist, illiberal political control of governments in many area of the world. Section 3 will test the hypotheses we have developed and provide insights into the ways in which civil servants cope with changes in their working environments.

3 Bureaucrats and Politicians in Three Selected Countries

We adopt a hybrid comparative approach, drawing on the logic of most-different systems designs (Przeworski and Teune 1982) while also recognizing key similarities across cases. Although Brazil, the United States, and the United Kingdom differ significantly in their institutional structures – such as presidential versus parliamentary systems, levels of bureaucratic insulation, and forms of political appointments – they have all experienced varying degrees of democratic backsliding in recent years. Part of the value of a most-different systems design is to identify common patterns even when many crucial characteristics are different (Anckar 2020).

At the same time, the variation in administrative traditions, state capacity, and bureaucratic autonomy allows us to explore how these factors condition responses to political pressures. Therefore, we will examine not only the general willingness of public servants in the three countries to resist political controls but also how individual characteristics interact with institutional constraints to shape bureaucratic resistance. By doing so, we contribute to the study of comparative public administration, provide a greater understanding of bureaucrats' individual-level attitudes, and inform broader debates on the role of bureaucracies in safeguarding democratic governance.

It may appear obvious that Brazil would be most different from the United States and the United Kingdom, but classifying the United States and the United Kingdom as most different systems may appear questionable to some readers. There have been a number of books and articles that deal with the two countries as being similar, largely based on a common heritage of political ideas. However, institutionally they differ in a number of ways, for example, federalism versus unitary government, presidential versus parliamentary, size, and so on.

Overall, the institutional and administrative structures of Brazil, the United States, and the United Kingdom present key differences that make them particularly relevant for comparative analysis. The United States relies on a highly politicized civil service at the upper echelons, where political appointees control key executive positions, often limiting the autonomy of career bureaucrats. The United Kingdom, by contrast, maintains a more professionalized and insulated civil service, where senior officials retain influence over policymaking while operating within a parliamentary system that prioritizes ministerial accountability. Brazil occupies an intermediate position: its bureaucracy is formally protected by a highly meritocratic and legalistic system, yet it remains vulnerable to political interference through discretionary appointments, particularly at leadership levels. These structural differences shape how bureaucrats in each country respond to political pressures and the extent to which they can resist undemocratic policies.

Beyond these structural distinctions, the role of bureaucratic autonomy and civil service protections varies significantly across the three countries. The UK's tradition of "serial loyalty" within its permanent civil service (Lodge 2010) contrasts with the US model, where career officials face greater risks of political retaliation, as evidenced by attempts to implement Schedule F under the Trump administration (Moynihan 2022). Brazil's public service, while enjoying strong job protections, has been subject to political co-optation, particularly through military appointments and external pressures exerted by the Bolsonaro administration (Lotta, Tavares, and Story 2024; Story, Lotta, and Tavares 2023). These institutional differences influence the mechanisms through which bureaucrats resist political encroachments – whether through formal policy advocacy, informal bureaucratic resistance, or strategic disengagement. By examining bureaucratic behavior in these distinct administrative contexts, this study provides broader insights into how public servants navigate political interference and safeguard democratic governance.

Broadly, all three countries passed through some degree of democratic backsliding in recent years. The extent of the backsliding, however, differs greatly. Consider, first, the status of their liberal democracy. We obtained data from the Varieties of Democracy project, which relies on expert surveys to track the level of democracy of most countries in the world. One of their indices, coordinated by Jan Teorell, is called the Liberal Democracy Index. Their manual explains it as follows:

> The liberal principle of democracy emphasizes the importance of protecting individual and minority rights against the tyranny of the state and the tyranny of the majority. The liberal model takes a 'negative' view of political power insofar as it judges the quality of democracy by the limits placed on government. This is achieved by constitutionally protected civil liberties, strong rule of law, an independent judiciary, and effective checks and balances that, together, limit the exercise of executive power. To make this a measure of liberal democracy, the index also takes the level of electoral democracy into account. (Coppedge 2024, 48)

The index varies from 0 (lowest) to 10 (highest) and covers a timeframe from 1789 to now. For the purposes of this Element, we selected the index assigned to the three countries in the most recent decades (2010–2023). We plotted them in Figure 1. Before we dig deeper into each case, we highlight some general trends. First, until 2015, the three countries enjoyed relatively high levels of liberal democracy. Both Brazil and the United States, but especially Brazil, struggled with a substantive decline in the following years and started recovering in the early 2020s. The United Kingdom, differently, enjoyed a slight improvement in the index between 2016–2018 and 2020, but saw a deterioration of its liberal democracy from 2020 to 2022. The years selected for our study regard moments when Brazil (2018–2019) and the United States (2020) were passing through a stark weakening of their democratic institutions, and when the United Kingdom (2020) was about to suffer with its starkest decay in the period.

In its 2019 report, the V-DEM Institute (2020) claimed that "the world is now evidently in a 'third wave of autocratization' (...). The number of citizens affected by autocratization surged from 415 million in 2016 to 2.3 billion in 2018." The surge, they explain, results not from a drastic increase in the number of autocratizing countries passing through this process, but because "three very populous countries (Brazil, India, and the United States) entered the group."

The deterioration in Brazil's liberal democracy began in 2016, when left-wing President Dilma Rousseff was removed from office. While the impeachment procedures followed due process, there has been an intense debate among scholars and the public on whether this was a coup (Marsteintredet and Malamud 2020). Her Vice-President Michel Temer took office with record-low

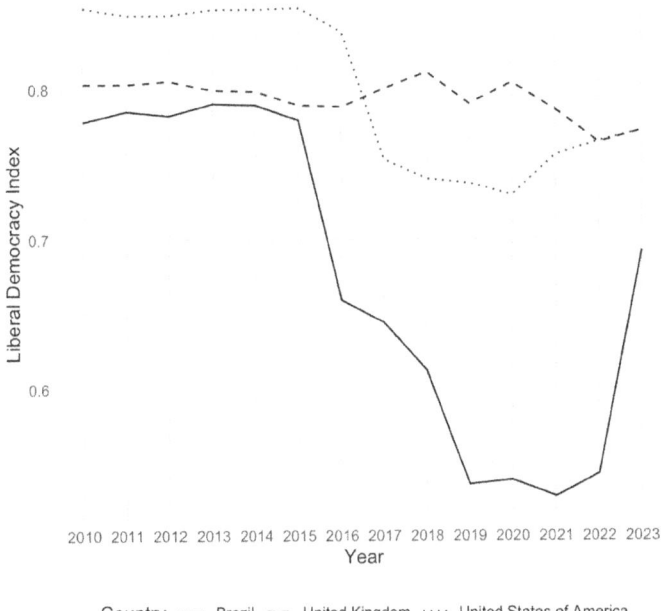

Figure 1 V-DEM's index of liberal democracy in three selected countries

popularity rates. In the following year, Mrs. Rousseff's co-partisan and former President Lula da Silva was arrested on corruption charges. He was released in 2019, when the lawsuits were canceled since the case's judge did not comply with due procedure. The judge, Sergio Moro, became Minister of Justice in the same year and was elected senator in 2022.

In 2018, one year after Lula's arrest, a highly polarized presidential election saw the victory of the far-right outsider Jair Bolsonaro. Often referred to as the "Trump of the Tropics" (Phillips 2018), Bolsonaro constantly attacked the media, democratic institutions, and the bureaucracy. Many of his strategies resembled those adopted by his American idol. This includes a riot on federal institutions on January 8, 2023, two years after Trump supporters attacked the Capitol.

The literature covering the relationship between Jair Bolsonaro and the federal public administration is bourgeoning. Like other elected officials, Bolsonaro appointed loyalists to work in several public agencies. In many cases, these were military personnel and retirees dedicated to enforcing the president's wishes. There are several reports of abusive behavior of political appointees (Story, Lotta, and Tavares 2023), leading not only to forced compliance but also the deterioration of career bureaucrats' self-efficacy (Lotta et al.

2024) and physical and mental health (Lotta, Tavares, and Story 2024). The presidency revisited entire regulations, for example, in the environmental arena (Bersch and Lotta 2023), and dismantled well-established policy sectors (Milhorance 2022; Sá e Silva 2020, 2022). Bureaucrats, willing to resist since Bolsonaro's election (Guedes-Neto and Peters 2021), reacted in several ways, including the reliance on international policy communities that exercised external pressure against the president's actions (Waisbich 2024).

The US decay is directly related to Donald Trump's attacks on the opposition, the media, and democratic institutions. He was elected president on November 8, 2016, and took office on January 20, 2017. From 2015 to 2017, the US's liberal democracy index declined 11.9% from 0.854 to 0.752. In 2020, when Trump left office, the index was 0.729. Since then, the index has risen to 0.772. This number is still lower if compared to the year when the illiberal leader was elected. This has to do with the constant attacks made by Trump and his growing followership, as well as acts of violence coordinated by his loyalists, including the attack on the Capitol in 2021.

The public administration literature shows several examples of how Trump's acts and attacks affected the civil service. The president and his staff often referred to the bureaucracy as the "Washington swamp" or the "deep state," his government passed through the longest federal shutdown in the country's history, and appointed Trump's family members for positions of influence (Moynihan and Roberts 2021). In fact, the former president signed an executive order in the end of his term allowing the replacement of a large number of merit-based personnel with patronage appointments. This proposition, labeled Schedule F, was revoked by Joe Biden. Otherwise, in the words of Moynihan (2022, 174), it "would have represented the most substantive change to the US civil service system since its creation in 1883."

In the current illiberal era, the United Kingdom is different in not having had a government that was clearly populist, as did Brazil and the United States. While some have styled Boris Johnson as a populist leader (Alexandre-Collier 2022; Lacatus and Meibauer 2022), he had little of the extreme rhetoric that characterized Donald Trump or Jair Bolsonaro. Likewise, the short stay in office of Liz Truss had some populist elements, but was too brief to have any appreciable impact. Therefore, civil service participants in our survey might be less sensitized to the possibilities of policy ideas that might violate fundamental legal principles, or threaten the rights of minorities.

However, the political landscape in the United Kingdom remained turbulent in 2020 and the subsequent years. The Prime Minister's Office and Parliament grappled with negotiations over the Brexit deal with the European Union. It was eventually ratified in 2020 after administrations led by both Theresa May and

Boris Johnson (with two governments each). Each prime minister served approximately three years, half the tenure of their predecessor, David Cameron, and much less than the ten years of Tony Blair. Liz Truss held office for fifty days in 2022 before being succeeded by Rishi Sunak. These events, among others, contributed to political uncertainty, shedding light on the UK's decline from 2020 to 2022 in the liberal democracy index.

Some of the decline in that index also may be attributed to the increased politicization of the civil service. That politicization has been in part is from the bottom up, with civil servants being more committed to policy issues (Hazell 2024) and willing to act on their commitments. Some of it has been more conventional top-down politicization, with politicians attempting to control their civil servants and to gain the loyalty of those charged with implementing the policies. Whatever the source, it does appear that the neutral civil service willing to exhibit "serial loyalty" may not be as robust an institution as it once was.

The selection of Brazil, the United States, and the United Kingdom provides theoretical and practical insights that extend beyond these cases, offering broader lessons on bureaucratic resistance in democratic backsliding. These countries represent distinct administrative traditions, levels of bureaucratic autonomy, and degrees of politicization, making them valuable for understanding how civil servants navigate political pressures in different institutional contexts.

The United States illustrates how a highly politicized bureaucracy, where senior positions are often filled by political appointees, can create vulnerabilities to executive influence but also opportunities for bureaucratic resistance through legal and procedural mechanisms. The United Kingdom, with its deeply embedded professional civil service, demonstrates how bureaucrats can leverage their institutional authority to influence policy continuity even amid political turbulence. Brazil, with its mix of strong civil service protections and political interference, highlights the role of informal networks and external alliances – such as engagement with international organizations – in resisting illiberal governance.

These cases, taken together, offer a comparative framework for analyzing bureaucratic resistance in other democracies facing similar pressures, from European countries grappling with rising populism to Latin American nations with volatile political landscapes. By identifying patterns of resistance and the institutional conditions that enable or constrain bureaucratic autonomy, this study provides valuable insights applicable to a wide range of democratic settings.

4 Empirical Tests

To test the hypotheses developed in the preceding sections, we have used survey experiments. We are less concerned in this research with the exit of civil servants but rather focus on shirking and sabotage (for studies on exit, see Guedes-Neto 2022; Schuster et al. 2021). Also, as well as testing the specific hypotheses about the possible causes of a willingness to shirk or sabotage, these data provide us with a general picture of the willingness of civil servants to engage in nontraditional behaviors when faced with "unprincipled principals." The methodology employed enables us to manipulate the stimuli given to respondents and to see under which conditions they may or may not be willing to resist the policy initiatives of their political superiors.

We conducted survey experiments to test our hypotheses, engaging a convenience sample of 942 public employees from the United States, the United Kingdom, and Brazil. While the sample sizes are relatively small within each country, we conducted power analyses demonstrating that they are sufficient to detect the treatment effects presented in our results. Additionally, we acknowledge that these samples are not fully representative of the bureaucracies in any of the three countries. This challenge is common in public administration research, as scholars often face difficulties in recruiting samples that accurately reflect the broader civil service, limiting the feasibility of fully representative cross-national comparisons. To mitigate these limitations, as we will further clarify, we incorporate a series of individual-level covariates to control for variation in demographic and professional characteristics across samples, enhancing the validity of our comparative analyses.

To recruit participants in the United States, we employed the services of Qualtrics, a firm specializing in subject recruitment through various survey companies. We implemented rigorous quality control measures to exclude respondents not affiliated with the public sector or those who exhibited insufficient attentiveness while completing the questionnaire. Fieldwork took place during the final week of the 2020 presidential election (October 27–30, 2020), resulting in 420 respondents representing diverse administrative branches, experience levels, and socio-demographic characteristics.

The British sample was recruited via Prolific, a platform renowned for its extensive participant pool, particularly in the United Kingdom. Participants underwent a comprehensive assessment of socio-demographic factors, allowing for targeted recruitment of individuals affiliated with the public service. Survey administration occurred from November 22–27, 2020, coinciding with the UK's imminent departure from the European Union. The final sample comprised 394 public employees, exhibiting a wide array of professional and personal backgrounds.

For the recruitment of Brazilian civil servants, we adopted a distinct approach. Given the absence of major survey firms specializing in the selection of bureaucrats, we collaborated with two municipal governments – one in the state of Minas Gerais and the other in Santa Catarina. These municipalities, with populations ranging from 70,000 to 90,000, boasted relatively high Human Development Index scores (0.7–0.8) and approximately 2,500 public employees each. The local government sent invitations to all civil servants possessing email addresses, who then volunteered to participate in the online, anonymous questionnaire in Portuguese. Fieldwork spanned from November 2018 to January 2019, shortly after the election of the far-right President Jair Bolsonaro, yielding a convenience sample of 128 bureaucrats.

The surveys were deliberately fielded during periods of heightened political tension in each country to capture bureaucratic attitudes when concerns about illiberal governance and democratic backsliding were most salient. In the United Kingdom, the survey coincided with the Brexit negotiations, a period of deep uncertainty for civil servants as political leaders challenged long-standing institutional norms. In the United States, data collection took place immediately following Trump's electoral defeat, when the administration was actively contesting election results and escalating rhetoric against the so-called "deep state." Meanwhile, in Brazil, the survey was conducted shortly after Bolsonaro's electoral victory, a moment when bureaucrats were beginning to assess the implications of his administration's governance style and potential threats to bureaucratic autonomy. By situating the surveys within these politically charged contexts, we maximize the relevance of our findings by capturing bureaucratic attitudes at moments when civil servants were most likely to be reflecting on their role in resisting or complying with illiberal policies.

While the surveys were conducted at different points in time, this intentional design choice enhances comparability rather than undermining it. Instead of capturing bureaucratic attitudes during routine governance, our study leverages periods of political turbulence as a natural setting for assessing resistance. Since democratic backsliding is inherently episodic – unfolding in response to political events rather than in a uniform manner across countries – our research design ensures that bureaucratic attitudes are measured when concerns about democratic erosion were at their peak. This approach strengthens the external validity of our findings by ensuring that our data reflect bureaucratic responses to real-world threats rather than abstract or hypothetical scenarios.

We present the descriptive statistics of our covariates in Table 1. Initially, age was categorized into eight groups,[6] with the average response indicating an age range between 39 and 45 years (average response: 4.215). Similarly, years of experience in the public sector were divided into eight categories,[7] with

---

[6] The age groups were: 18–24 (1); 25–31 (2); 32–38 (3); 39–45 (4); 46–52 (5); 53–59 (6); 60–66 (7); and 67 or older (8).
[7] The experience groups were: Less than 1 year (0); 1–5 (1); 6–10 (2); 11–15 (3); 16–20 (4); 21–25 (5); 26–30 (6); and more than 30 years (7).

Table 1 Descriptive statistics: Covariates

Variable	Mean	Std. Dev.	Min	Max
Age	4.215	1.736	1	8
Experience	2.926	1.973	0	7
Education	2.029	1.201	0	4
Male	0.367	0.482	0	1
Appointee	0.083	0.276	0	1
Supervision	0.387	0.487	0	1
Tenure	0.434	0.496	0	1
Discretion	5.775	2.602	0	10

category 2 representing 6–10 years and category 3 representing 11–15 years. Regarding education, respondents had the option to select from various levels, including high school or less (1), vocational education (2), bachelor's degree (3), professional postgraduation (4), and academic postgraduation (5), with the average respondent holding a bachelor's degree (2.029).

Table 1 displays four binary variables: gender (36.7% male), political appointee (8.3%), supervisor (38.7%), and tenure (43.4%). Additionally, respondents were queried about the level of autonomy they experience in their daily work, with an average score of 5.775 on a scale from 0 to 10. Overall, our sample is characterized by considerable experience and education, with a notable proportion holding supervisory positions.

Participants were also asked about their branch of work, with the majority indicating the executive branch (76.6%), followed by the legislative (13.4%) and the judiciary (7.7%). A small percentage (2.2%) did not select any of these branches. Furthermore, respondents were queried about their administrative level, categorized as high (e.g., federal level in the United States, central government in the United Kingdom), mid (e.g., state level in the United States, devolved government in the United Kingdom), and local. The majority of respondents indicated working at the local level (49.7%), particularly notable in the Brazilian sample, which exclusively comprised such participants. This was followed by high (26.6%) and mid-administrative levels (21.9%). While this distribution may not be representative of the public sector in the selected countries, we anticipate meaningful responses given the randomized distribution of respondents and the varied stimuli introduced through survey experiments.

Notable differences exist among the samples from the three countries. In summary, the US sample tends to be older (mean of 4.96, compared to 3.32 in Brazil), more experienced (3.29, compared to 2.42 in Brazil), and has a higher proportion of male respondents (41.7% compared to 22.7% in Brazil). Conversely, the Brazilian sample exhibits a higher prevalence of tenured bureaucrats (79.7%, compared to 27.2% in the United Kingdom) and political appointees (28.9%, compared to 4.8% in the United States and the United Kingdom), as well as a higher level of education (mean of 2.41, compared to 1.79 in the United Kingdom).

While these differences may raise concerns when comparing the samples, our analysis demonstrates that the results remain consistent even after accounting for key covariates, including demographic and professional characteristics. This robustness check increases our confidence that the observed patterns are not merely artifacts of sample composition but instead reflect common underlying trends in bureaucratic attitudes across the three countries. Despite differences in institutional structures and survey timing, the stability of our findings suggests that bureaucrats in these contexts respond in systematically comparable ways to political pressures, reinforcing the validity of our cross-national analysis.

4.1 List Experiments

Shirking and sabotage by civil servants are often deemed undesirable behaviors in normative terms (Pierre and Peters 2017). Public workers generally have been observed preferring to do at least some work rather than none. This is especially true if we consider the findings of research on public service motivation (see Perry 1997) that indicates that in most settings civil servants are committed to their jobs Furthermore, in many cases, not working may go against the bureaucrat's professional code of conduct, therefore risking different kinds of punishment: a lower salary, in agencies that adopt a pay-for-performance system, fewer chances for promotions, or even the employee's dismissal. These multiple possibilities will likely produce a social desirability bias in any survey responses related to working and sabotage.

Given the potential lack of sincerity in respondents' self-reporting regarding the consideration of adopting such strategies, direct questioning is deemed unlikely to produce reliable results. To mitigate social desirability bias, we employ a list experiment, as recommended by Peters and Guedes-Neto (2020), which allows subjects to avoid directly admitting to holding controversial positions or behaviors while still enabling researchers to draw inferences about such behaviors and attitudes. Several authors validated the benefits of list experiments in contexts of high social desirability bias (Gonzales-Ocantos et al. 2012; Oliveros 2016). Gonzalez-Ocantos et al. (2012), for example, demonstrate that voters will lie if asked directly about vote-buying but will be sincere if the question is part of a list experiment.

The list experiment, also known as the item count technique, was originally introduced by Miller (1984) in her doctoral dissertation as a method to elicit truthful responses to sensitive survey questions while minimizing social desirability bias. Since then, it has become a widely used and well-validated method in political science and survey research. A meta-analysis by Blair, Coppock, and Moor (2020) reviewed nearly 300 studies spanning 30 years and confirmed that list experiments provide a robust and reliable means of estimating the prevalence of sensitive behaviors or attitudes, particularly when the underlying assumptions – such as no design effects and truthful reporting – hold.

The logic of the list experiment is straightforward. Respondents are randomly assigned to either a control or treatment condition. Those in the control group receive a list of four nonsensitive items and are asked to indicate how many of those items apply to them, without specifying which ones. The treatment group, in contrast, receives the same four items with the addition of a fifth, potentially sensitive item. Respondents in both groups report only the total number of items they endorse, preserving anonymity regarding their response to the sensitive item. Because random assignment ensures that any preexisting differences between the groups are distributed equally, the difference in the mean number of endorsed items between the treatment and control groups provides an unbiased estimate of the proportion of respondents selecting the sensitive item (Sniderman et al. 2011).

This methodology is particularly useful in contexts where respondents may be reluctant to disclose sensitive views or behaviors due to fear of judgment, political pressure, or legal concerns. Unlike direct questioning, which can introduce sensitivity bias, the list experiment mitigates this risk by making it impossible to determine an individual respondent's answer to the sensitive question, thus encouraging more honest responses. Furthermore, the difference-in-means estimator used in list experiments has been extensively validated in the literature, demonstrating its robustness even when response ranges differ between conditions.

In our initial list experiment, we regard shirking as a proxy for resistance. Subjects allocated to the control condition encounter the following vignette:

> The following four scenarios are common in public departments around the world. There is evidence that some of these scenarios demotivate several civil servants, leading them to dedicate less effort than they would dedicate to other activities. For instance, they may try to assign another colleague to do these tasks, they may do them partially, miss deadlines, or do not do them.
>
> A civil servant was assigned to work in a project that . . .
>
> - is very similar to every other project that she/he has always worked at.
> - favors only her/his own political group.

- is entirely new to her/him, requiring training and additional efforts.
- creates a political advantage to groups that she/he is against.

In the treatment condition, participants received the same text as the control group, supplemented with a fifth item: "it reduces citizens' political rights, such as the freedom of expression or press." Subsequently, all participants were prompted with the question: "In your opinion, how many of the previous scenarios would lead a standard civil servant to dedicate fewer efforts to the project in comparison to other activities? Please, answer only with the number of scenarios." Response options ranged from 0 to 4 in the control condition and 0 to 5 in the treatment condition.

Three theoretical considerations guided our experimental design. Firstly, to further alleviate social desirability bias associated with shirking, respondents were encouraged to consider a "standard civil servant." This approach, as suggested by Mutz (2011), allows subjects to express their perceptions without directly admitting to potentially politically incorrect behaviors.

Secondly, to mitigate measurement error arising from extreme responses (0 or 4), we carefully selected control items with negative correlations, ensuring that respondents would be less likely to endorse all or none of the listed options. For instance, it is improbable for someone selecting "is very similar to every other project that she/he has always worked at" to also choose "is entirely new to her/him, requiring training and additional efforts." This structuring reduces the likelihood of flooring and ceiling effects, which can bias estimates by artificially constraining variation in responses (Glynn 2013).

By implementing this strategy effectively, we anticipated an average response in the control condition of approximately 2, meaning that respondents would endorse some – but not all – items, thereby improving the precision of our estimate of the sensitive item's prevalence. A well-balanced distribution of responses ensures that the difference-in-means estimator remains unbiased, as extreme response clustering (all 0s or all 4s) could otherwise distort the estimation of treatment effects.

Thirdly, to further prevent flooring effects, we included at least one high-likelihood item, namely "creates a political advantage to groups that she/he is against." Given the nature of political dynamics in bureaucratic environments, we anticipated that this item would receive broad agreement among respondents, thereby reducing the likelihood of zero endorsements across the entire control group. This design choice aligns with Kuklinski et al. (1997), who demonstrated that including at least one widely endorsed item stabilizes variance and improves estimator reliability. Together, these methodological choices ensure that our list experiment adheres to best practices, maximizing the accuracy of our treatment effect estimates while minimizing distortions caused by extreme response patterns.

Our subsequent experiment, focusing on the possibility of sabotage, mirrored the previous one. The options and survey questions remained unchanged, while the introductory text read as follows:

> Now, consider the possibility of undermining a project. A common reaction in different public departments is that some civil servants decide to work against a project to which they were assigned to work at. In other words, instead of implementing it, they decide to do whatever they can so that the project does not move forward.

To summarize the key differences, while both experiments investigate bureaucratic resistance, they capture distinct forms of noncompliance. The first experiment, centered on shirking, examines bureaucrats who choose to withdraw effort or passively disengage from implementing a project assigned to them. This is reflected in the introductory text, which emphasizes civil servants who neglect their responsibilities rather than actively obstructing a policy. In contrast, the second experiment focuses on sabotage, a more deliberate and proactive form of resistance, where bureaucrats intentionally undermine a project to ensure its failure. The introductory text in this case explicitly frames the scenario as one in which public employees work against a project rather than merely failing to contribute to its execution. By maintaining consistent response options while altering the framing of resistance, the design allows us to compare bureaucratic behaviors along a continuum from passive to active resistance.

Following the data collection phase, we conducted data analysis using two-way t-tests to compare differences in means. Our underlying assumption, once again, is that the randomization process effectively neutralized any effects that could be attributed to other covariates (Peters and Guedes-Neto 2020). Additionally, we performed post-hoc power analyses to evaluate the statistical reliability of our findings, ensuring that only results with a minimum power of 0.80 were considered robust enough for interpretation (Bausell and Li 2006). While a priori power analysis is crucial in experimental designs to determine the required sample size beforehand, post-hoc power analysis serves an equally important role in studies with fixed or convenience samples, where researchers must assess whether observed effects are adequately powered (Perugini, Gallucci, and Costantini 2018). This approach allows us to filter out potentially underpowered results, reducing the risk of Type II errors and ensuring that our conclusions are drawn from statistically meaningful effects.

The balance table is presented in Table 2. Notably, the only variable that is not balanced across conditions is discretion. To address this and account for other

Table 2 Balance table

Variable	Control	Treatment	P-value (DoM)
Age	4.236	4.195	0.718
Experience	2.924	2.927	0.982
Education	2.063	1.994	0.374
Male	0.373	0.362	0.733
Appointee	0.080	0.086	0.753
Supervision	0.368	0.407	0.227
Tenure	0.451	0.418	0.308
Discretion	5.537	6.017	0.005
Salary	1.461	1.443	0.740
Branch	1.299	1.347	0.313
Level	2.236	2.298	0.278

Note: The groups represent the subjects that were randomized for the list experiments. "*P*-value (DoM)" regards the *p*-value of the two-way *t*-test based on the difference of means.

potential omitted variables, we conducted a series of robustness checks as we further explain in the following sections.

4.2 Heterogeneous Treatment Effects

Our theoretical framework requires the assessment of heterogeneous treatment effects, indicating experimental outcomes that vary based on respondent characteristics. Initially, we explore variations in treatment effects by country, dividing the sample into three groups: the United States, United Kingdom, and Brazil, and conducting individual two-way *t*-tests for each case. Again, we are cautious with cross-country comparisons because our samples are not nationally representative of each country's bureaucracy.

Subsequently, we investigate treatment effects based on respondents' perceptions of opportunities in the private sector. Our H_2 posited that *those civil servants who believe that they would be (financially) better off in the private sector will be more likely to resist undemocratic policies*. Respondents were prompted to envision a scenario where a civil servant, possessing equivalent experience and contacts to their own, opts to seek employment in the private sector. Among the 942 respondents, 66.56% anticipated a higher salary in the private sector, 12.10% expected the same salary, and the remaining 21.34% anticipated a lower salary. To test H_2, we dichotomize responses into two categories: (1) anticipation of a higher salary in the private sector and (2) expectation of the same or lower salary.

For testing H$_3$ (the effect of tenure) and H$_4$ (the effects of supervisory responsibilities), our categorization approach is more straightforward. We differentiate between respondents who are tenured and those who are not for H$_3$, and for H$_4$, we distinguish between supervisors and subordinates. Given our lack of hypothesized country differences in heterogeneous treatment effects for these individual-level categorizations, we solely test them based on the entire sample. This methodological decision is also influenced by our sample size, which would be substantially reduced if we attempted to select, for instance, only tenured individuals from specific countries.

5 Findings

5.1 H$_1$: Are Bureaucrats Willing to Shirk and Sabotage?

We present our baseline results in Tables 3 and 4. Before interpreting the treatment effects, we emphasize three key points warranting special attention. Firstly, the average response in the control condition closely approximates two, validating our empirical design. Secondly, across all cases, the p-value is below 0.05 and the statistical power exceeds 0.80. As per professional standards, these thresholds signify statistical significance in the difference of means. Thirdly, as previously explained, our focus lies on the disparity of means between the control and treatment conditions, indicating respondents who selected the fifth statement unique to the treatment condition (i.e., the undemocratic scenario).

While we anticipate resistance among bureaucrats regardless of country (H$_1$), we expect to observe heightened intent to resist in Brazil, followed by the United Kingdom and the United States (in this sequence). Our findings corroborate this hypothesis, supporting H$_1$ and aligning with our comparative expectations. American civil servants exhibit the lowest inclination towards shirking or sabotage, yet they still demonstrate a notable willingness to resist. Regarding

Table 3 Are bureaucrats willing to shirk?

	Pooled data	United States	United Kingdom	Brazil
Control	1.935 [475]	1.953 [211]	1.908 [196]	1.956 [68]
Treatment	2.582 [467]	2.541 [209]	2.561 [198]	2.800 [60]
Difference	0.648 [942]	0.588 [420]	0.652 [394]	0.844 [128]
P-value	0.001	0.001	0.001	0.001
Power	1.000	1.000	1.000	0.984

Note: Average response and, between brackets, sample size. Results of two-sample t-test. Statistical power is computed with an alpha of 0.05.

Table 4 Are bureaucrats willing to sabotage?

	Pooled data	United States	United Kingdom	Brazil
Control	1.453 [475]	1.550 [211]	1.270 [196]	1.676 [68]
Treatment	2.143 [467]	2.148 [209]	1.965 [198]	2.717 [60]
Difference	0.691 [942]	0.599 [420]	0.694 [394]	1.040 [128]
P-value	0.001	0.001	0.001	0.001
Power	1.000	0.999	1.000	0.998

Note: Average response and, between brackets, sample size. Results of two-sample *t*-test. Statistical power is computed with an alpha of 0.05.

shirking (Table 3), 58.8% of US respondents assert that a standard civil servant would consider shirking if tasked with implementing a policy contrary to basic democratic rights. This sentiment is even more pronounced among British (65.2%) and Brazilian (84.4%) bureaucrats. Comparable results are observed for sabotage: 59.9% among American respondents compared to 69.4% among those in the UK sample and the whole treated sample for Brazil.

The difference between the treatment effects of the US and UK samples is less than 0.10 in both instances. Furthermore, they never surpass the 70% mark. These figures noticeably contrast with the outcomes observed in the experiments conducted in Brazil. In this developing country, 84.4% of respondents believe their peers would be inclined to shirk if tasked with implementing undemocratic policies, and even more strikingly, 104.0% indicate a potential willingness to sabotage the government. The latter result surpasses the 1.00 mark, suggesting a triggering effect that prompts respondents to demonstrate a readiness to engage in sabotage in other contexts as well when exposed to the undemocratic frame.

5.2 H_2: Does the Perception of Better Opportunities in the Private Sector Affect Resistance?

Next, we examine the influence of perceived opportunities in the private sector on the willingness to resist undemocratic policies. We hypothesize that individuals who perceive better opportunities in the private sector will demonstrate a greater propensity to shirk and sabotage compared to others. Our data substantiate this hypothesis. As depicted in Table 5, 69.6% of respondents who anticipate better salaries in the private sector also believe their peers would shirk if tasked with implementing an undemocratic policy. In contrast, this figure stands at 55.1% among those who expect similar or inferior earnings in the private sector.

Table 5 Perceived salary and resistance

	Shirking		Sabotage	
	Better in private	Worse or same	Better in private	Worse or same
Control	1.902 [316]	2.000 [159]	1.399 [316]	1.560 [159]
Treatment	2.598 [311]	2.551 [156]	2.112 [311]	2.205 [156]
Difference	0.696 [627]	0.551 [315]	0.714 [627]	0.645 [315]
P-value	0.001	0.001	0.001	0.001
Power	1.000	0.980	1.000	0.994

Note: Average response and, between brackets, sample size. Results of two-sample *t*-test. Statistical power is computed with an alpha of 0.05.

Similarly, the list experiment investigating sabotage as a form of resistance yields analogous results. Among those perceiving superior opportunities in the private sector, 71.4% believe that standard civil servants would engage in sabotage when confronted with policies undermining freedom of expression and the press. Conversely, only 64.5% of those not anticipating higher salaries in the private sector hold the same expectation.

To reaffirm, all treatment effects exhibit considerable magnitude. In each scenario, over half of the treated individuals expressed their intent to shirk or sabotage if tasked with implementing an undemocratic policy. This holds true regardless of whether individuals perceive themselves as underpaid or overpaid. However, there is a notable escalation in treatment effects among those anticipating higher earnings in the private sector.

5.3 H_3: Do Tenured Bureaucrats Differ from Untenured Public Employees?

Our subsequent hypothesis posits that tenured public employees are more inclined to shirk and sabotage compared to noncareer bureaucrats. However, our findings fail to support this assertion. Table 6 illustrates the results for shirking, revealing virtually identical differences in means for both tenured (0.649) and untenured civil servants (0.640). Contrary to our hypothesis, there appears to be no significant disparity in propensity to shirk between these two groups.

Additionally, we present the heterogeneous treatment effects of the sabotage experiment within the same table. Surprisingly, the results contradict our hypothesis; 71.9% of the untenured respondents believe their peers would be inclined to sabotage, whereas this sentiment is shared by only 66.0% of the tenured portion of the sample. This unexpected finding suggests that tenure

Table 6 Tenure and resistance

	Shirking		Sabotage	
	Tenured	**Untenured**	**Tenured**	**Untenured**
Control	1.874 [214]	1.985 [261]	1.509 [214]	1.406 [261]
Treatment	2.523 [195]	2.625 [272]	2.169 [195]	2.125 [272]
Difference	0.649 [409]	0.640 [533]	0.660 [409]	0.719 [533]
P-value	0.001	0.001	0.001	0.001
Power	1.000	1.000	1.000	1.000

Note: Average response and, between brackets, sample size. Results of two-sample *t*-test. Statistical power is computed with an alpha of 0.05.

status may not be a decisive factor in predicting willingness to engage in sabotage.

The heightened inclination of untenured bureaucrats to engage in sabotage compared to their tenured counterparts may arise from various factors, including perceived job insecurity, limited exposure to consequences, and a desire to assert dedication to democratic principles. For instance, some untenured public employees might view their tenure in government as transitory, prioritizing the cultivation of a pro-democracy reputation over compromising their democratic values. Additionally, they may be more tolerant of being labeled as saboteurs by colleagues, recognizing their temporary status within the organization as a buffer against the potential repercussions of a tarnished reputation.

Conversely, both tenured and untenured bureaucrats demonstrate similar propensities to shirk, indicating that the influences on shirking behavior may diverge from those affecting sabotage tendencies. These findings underscore the intricate interplay of job security, experience with consequences, and career aspirations in shaping employee conduct within bureaucratic settings, with tenure status exerting distinct effects on the inclination to engage in acts of resistance versus avoidance of work-related duties.

5.4 H_4: Do Supervisors Differ from Subordinates?

Our final hypothesis posits that subordinates will demonstrate a greater willingness to resist than their supervisors. The findings from the combined datasets substantiate our hypothesis at standard levels of significance and power, as shown in Table 7. Specifically, our analysis reveals that 60.9% of supervisors believe that a standard civil servant would shirk in the face of an undemocratic policy. This treatment effect escalates to 67.9% among subordinates alone.

Table 7 Supervisory status and shirking

	Shirking		Sabotage	
	Supervisors	**Subordinates**	**Supervisors**	**Subordinates**
Control	1.886 [175]	1.963 [300]	1.400 [175]	1.483 [300]
Treatment	2.495 [190]	2.643 [277]	2.016 [190]	2.231 [277]
Difference	0.609 [365]	0.679 [577]	0.616 [365]	0.748 [577]
P-value	0.001	0.001	0.001	0.001
Power	0.998	1.000	0.997	1.000

Note: Average response and, between brackets, sample size. Results of two-sample *t*-test. Statistical power is computed with an alpha of 0.05.

The disparity between groups is even more pronounced for sabotage. While 61.6% of supervisors are keen to sabotage, a notable 74.8% of respondents without supervisory status expect this form of democratic resistance. Thus, our results consistently support the hypothesis that subordinates exhibit a greater propensity to resist compared to their superiors in both scenarios.

It's noteworthy that while the disparity in treatment effects is 7 percentage points in the shirking experiment, it widens to 13.2 percentage points when respondents are queried about sabotage. This indicates that closeness to the agency's leadership acts as a more substantial deterrent to sabotage than to shirking. Subordinates demonstrate a greater propensity to opt for the most radical alternative – sabotage – compared to shirking, such as deliberately missing deadlines. In essence, bureaucrats who maintain a distance from political leaders exhibit a clear willingness to confront undemocratic officials.

5.5 Does Peer Pressure Affect Bureaucratic Response?

We crafted the list experiment to minimize the influence of social desirability bias, ensuring respondents could express their willingness to resist undemocratic policies freely. Nevertheless, real-life settings entail inherent costs. For instance, Pierre and Peters (2017) assert that peer pressure often compels bureaucrats to prioritize work over shirking. To address this, we posed a follow-up question to subjects from the United States and the United Kingdom: "Would your answer have been the same if you knew that most work colleagues would disagree with what you answered?" Responses ranged from "It would definitely change" (0) to "It would definitely remain the same" (10). Our results reveal that the majority of public employees perceive minimal influence from peer pressure, as depicted in the histogram plotted in Figure 2.

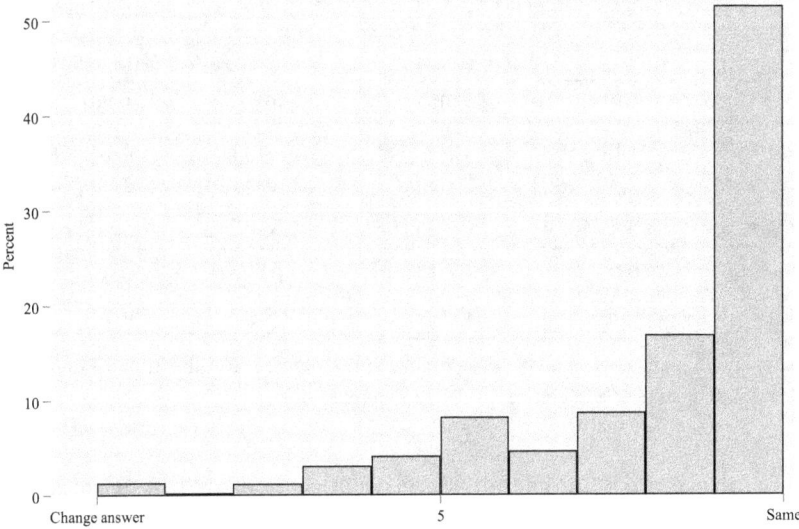

Figure 2 Histogram: Would the respondent's answer remain the same if colleagues disagree?

Analyzing our sample, we observed that 38.21% of respondents chose 10, and 68.31% selected at least 8 (i.e., from 10 to 8), indicating a prevailing perception of low costs associated with peer pressure. None of the other categories (7 and below) was chosen by more than 9% of the respondents. Since there seems to be a significant difference between the subsamples choosing 8 or more on one side, and 7 or less on the other, we created a dummy variable categorizing respondents into these two groups. We refer to the first group (8–10) as those who perceive low costs of peer pressure, while the second (0–7) perceives high costs. We then conducted two-way t-tests to assess the treatment effects among each of these groups.

The treatment effects of the shirking experiment are presented in Table 8. We find that even among those who would not be willing to change their response (*low-cost perception*), there is still a significant number of bureaucrats who would be willing to shirk. The treatment effects in the low perception category are 54% in the United States and 67% in the United Kingdom. Based on these findings, we propose a conservative estimation of the share of bureaucrats that would be willing to shirk regardless of peer pressure (at least in our convenience sample). In the United States, these are the 54% identified in the list experiment among the 74.76% of the sample, which is in the low perception category, yielding 40.37% $[0.54 \times 0.7476 = 0.4037]$ of the American respondents. In the United Kingdom, this is 67% of 61.42% of the sample, that is, 41.15% $[0.67 \times 0.6142 = 0.4115]$.

Table 8 Shirking depending on the perceived costs of peer pressure

	United States		United Kingdom	
	Low	High	Low	High
Control	1.96 [165]	1.93 [46]	1.74 [118]	2.17 [78]
Treatment	2.50 [149]	2.65 [60]	2.40 [124]	2.82 [74]
Difference	0.54 [314]	0.72 [106]	0.67 [242]	0.66 [152]
P-value	0.01	0.01	0.01	0.01
Power	0.99	0.95	0.99	0.93

Note: Average response and, between brackets, sample size. Results of two-sample *t*-test. Statistical power is computed with an alpha of 0.05.

To recap, our most flexible estimation, which considers only treatment effects among those with a low-cost perception of peer pressure, supports our cross-country expectation that British bureaucrats (67%) are more willing to resist than those from the United States (54%). Our conservative estimation, which accounts for the share of respondents who see low costs in peer pressure, produces only a very small difference across countries: 41.2% (United Kingdom) and 40.4% (United States).

We present the results for sabotage in Table 9. We find that among those who are not responsive to peer pressure, this starker type of resistance is even more likely to exist both in the United States (55%) and the United Kingdom (82%). Following the same strategy proposed in the previous paragraph, we estimate that 41.12% $[0.55 \times 0.7476 = 0.4112]$ of the American public employees who participated in our experiment believe that sabotage would take place in case of implementing an undemocratic policy. This compares to 50.36% $[0.82 \times 0.6142 = 0.5036]$ of the British sample. These estimations support our cross-national that it is more likely to identify resistance in the United Kingdom than in the United States regardless of the measurement strategy.

In addition to the cross-national comparisons, even our most conservative estimations yield a compelling result: a substantive share of participants demonstrates a readiness to resist undemocratic policies. This finding not only reinforces H_1 but also underscores the pivotal role of bureaucrats as core veto actors within democratic backsliding processes. It emphasizes the potential influence wielded by civil servants in safeguarding democratic principles and resisting illiberal leaders, thereby highlighting the critical importance of understanding and engaging with bureaucratic perspectives in efforts to uphold and fortify democratic institutions.

Table 9 Sabotage depending on the perceived costs of peer pressure

	United States		United Kingdom	
	Low	High	Low	High
Control	1.52 [165]	1.65 [46]	1.06 [118]	1.59 [78]
Treatment	2.07 [149]	2.33 [60]	1.88 [124]	2.11 [74]
Difference	0.55 [314]	0.68 [106]	0.82 [242]	0.52 [152]
P-value	0.01	0.01	0.01	0.02
Power	0.98	0.79	1.00	0.68

Note: Average response and, between brackets, sample size. Results of two-sample *t*-test. Statistical power is computed with an alpha of 0.05.

5.6 Vignette Experiment

In addition to our list experiment, we employed a second strategy to address any potentially unrealistic perceptions of decision costs among respondents. Following their response to a series of initial questions, participants were randomly assigned to one of two groups and exposed to a vignette experiment. To ensure unbiased results, we implemented two key measures. Firstly, we exposed participants to a series of survey questions between the list experiment and the vignette experiment. These functioned as confounders, thus minimizing any potential bias. Secondly, we re-randomized all subjects upon entry into the vignette experiment, ensuring an equal chance of assignment to either the control or treatment conditions. The vignette presented to participants was structured as follows:

> Paul is a civil servant. Recently, he was assigned to work in a project which he disagrees with. According to Paul, this project *[Control: "does not reduce"] [Treatment: "reduces"]* the freedom of expression and press of the population *[Control: "population, but"] [Treatment: "population and"]* it is a terrible policy for the country."
>
> Using his autonomy, Paul decided to not carry out his tasks related to this project.
>
> If you were in Paul's shoes, what is the probability that you would have not carried out your tasks related to this project as well?
>
> Please, use the 0–10 scale, where 0 means "very improbable" and 10 "very probable."

While a vignette experiment inherently carries a higher risk of inducing social desirability bias compared to a list experiment (Peters and Guedes-Neto 2020), we incorporated additional measures to introduce a nuanced understanding of decision costs. Firstly, we modified the wording to heighten the perceived stakes: rather than referencing a generic "standard civil servant," respondents were prompted to consider their own behavior. More importantly, we crafted a vignette

Table 10 Vignette experiment: Are bureaucrats willing to shirk?

	Pooled data	United States	United Kingdom	Brazil
Control	3.158 [438]	2.898 [177]	2.798 [197]	4.984 [64]
Treatment	4.085 [504]	4.041 [243]	3.741 [197]	5.312 [64]
Difference	0.928 [942]	1.143 [420]	0.944 [394]	0.328 [128]
P-value	0.001	0.001	0.001	0.575
Power	0.998	0.983	0.926	0.087

Note: Average response and, between brackets, sample size. Results of two-sample t-test. Statistical power is computed with an alpha of 0.05.

that could effectively differentiate between the effects of an undemocratic policy and those of a policy perceived as democratic but personally disliked by the respondent. This deliberate design enables us to pinpoint the specific willingness to resist undemocratic leaders, shedding light on the nuanced dynamics of bureaucratic decision-making under varying policy contexts.

Our results are presented in Table 10. In the pooled sample, we find that those respondents who were treated are, on average, more willing to shirk than those in the control condition at a rate of change of 29.35% [(4.085 − 3.158)/3.158]. This finding still supports our expectation that bureaucrats are willing to resist undemocratic policies more than other policies that are undesirable yet democratic.

Here, we also find that the treatment effects are slightly higher among American bureaucrats than among those in the United Kingdom, suggesting either that British respondents were more influenced by social desirability bias or that part of the effects captured in the list experiment were not exclusively related to the undemocratic character of the policy. To be more precise, this suggests that resistance in Britain (compared to the United States) is more likely to occur for reasons that go beyond sustaining democracy.

Furthermore, we do not find any statistically significant effect in the Brazilian sample. This may be caused either by the small sample size or a lack of interest in resisting undemocratic policies compared to policies that Brazilian public employees dislike even though they are democratic. The latter proposition appears to be the case, considering that the average of the control group is considerably higher in Brazil than in all other countries – in the control group, the average in the Brazilian sample is 4.98 compared to 2.80 in the United Kingdom and 2.90 in the United States. That is, even when the policy is not undemocratic, our subjects appear to be more willing to shirk than in the United Kingdom and the United States.

5.7 Omitted Variable Bias and Balance across Countries

In the balance table (see Table 2), we show that our randomization process was successful at assigning similar samples to the two experimental conditions. This allows us to affirm that our experiment is unlikely to have been influenced by omitted variable bias (Mutz 2011), thus justifying the use of two-way t-tests. However, one variable (*discretion*) was not balanced across groups. On average, those in the treatment group enjoy slightly more autonomy in their work when compared to participants assigned to the control condition.

To account for that and any other effect that does not derive from the treatment, we ran a multivariate OLS regression considering the outcome as the dependent variable, the treatment as the independent variable, and all the covariates collected in the survey (see Table 11). This strategy also helps to mitigate any differences that are caused by the different recruitment strategies employed in the three countries.

Table 11 OLS regressions controlling for multiple covariates

	List: Shirk	**List: Sabotage**	**Vignette: Shirk**
Treatment (List: Shirk)	0.653***	–	–
	(8.99)		
Treatment (List: Sabotage)	–	0.697***	–
		(9.02)	
Treatment (Vignette: Shirk)	–	–	0.970***
			(5.22)
Age	−0.100***	−0.093**	−0.144*
	(−3.58)	(−3.26)	(−1.96)
Male	0.055	0.163	0.297
	(0.69)	(1.93)	(1.50)
Political Appointee	−0.025	−0.005	0.160
	(−0.16)	(−0.04)	(0.40)
Supervisor	−0.112	−0.142	−0.026
	(−1.43)	(−1.74)	(−0.13)
Tenure	−0.119	0.012	0.150
	(−1.40)	(0.14)	(0.72)
Discretion	0.004	−0.004	0.051
	(0.25)	(−0.21)	(1.29)

Table 11 (cont.)

	List: Shirk	List: Sabotage	Vignette: Shirk
Education	−0.038	−0.069*	0.082
	(−1.23)	(−2.18)	(1.01)
Experience	0.014	0.002	−0.059
	(0.60)	(0.06)	(−1.03)
Salary (B: Lower in private sector)			
Same in private sector	0.075	0.162	0.022
	(0.53)	(1.08)	(0.06)
Higher in private sector	0.031	0.056	−0.413
	(0.31)	(0.56)	(−1.60)
Branch (B: Executive)			
Other	−0.201	0.136	−0.334
	(−0.72)	(0.63)	(−0.73)
Judiciary	0.006	0.201	0.025
	(0.04)	(1.28)	(0.07)
Legislative	−0.148	0.158	0.499
	(−1.47)	(1.35)	(1.81)
Level (B: High)			
Mid	0.020	0.077	0.372
	(0.19)	(0.64)	(1.33)
Local	0.070	0.167	0.514*
	(0.72)	(1.67)	(2.21)
Other	−0.272	−0.259	1.700*
	(−1.14)	(−0.95)	(2.38)
Country (B: Brazil)			
United States	−0.003	−0.173	−0.954*
	(−0.02)	(−1.15)	(−2.37)
United Kingdom	−0.146	−0.531***	−1.364***
	(−1.02)	(−3.58)	(−3.52)
Constant	1.810***	1.400***	3.147***
	(7.32)	(5.65)	(4.81)
Observations	942	942	942
R^2	0.104	0.130	0.098
Adjusted R^2	0.086	0.112	0.080

Note: t statistics in parentheses. * $p < 0.05$, ** $p < 0.01$, and *** $p < 0.001$.

Table 12 Average treatment effects based on the inverse-probability weighting (IPW) approach including all covariates

	List: Shirk	List: Sabotage	Vignette: Shirk
Treatment (List: Shirk)	0.647*** (0.072)	–	–
Treatment (List: Sabotage)	–	0.699*** (0.077)	–
Treatment (Vignette: Shirk)	–	–	0.965*** (0.184)
Observations	942	942	942

Note: Robust standard errors in parentheses. $^{*}p < 0.05$, $^{**}p < 0.01$, and $^{***}p < 0.001$. The same covariates of Table 11 are included but omitted from the results.

Furthermore, we adopted the inverse-probability weights (IPW) technique (see Table 12), a considerably more conservative estimation approach to calculate the average treatment effects. In short, it relies on weighted probabilities to correct missing data (Cattaneo 2010). In all cases, they are virtually the same as those presented in Tables 2 and 3 (pooled sample).

We use Imai and Ratkovic's (2014) test of overidentifying conditions to assess whether our IPW approach adequately fixed our estimations. We find support for the hypothesis that the treatment models balanced the covariates (p-value < 0.001). In other words, our results do not seem to derive from a lack of balance across treatment and control conditions or differences in the demographic or professional differences of subjects from the three countries.

We adopted the same IPW technique to compare average treatment effects across countries. That is, since the different recruitment approaches led to some differences in the characteristics of respondents from the United States, the United Kingdom, and Brazil, it is important to make sure that any effects are driven by the treatments and country of origin, and not by other covariates (e.g., tenure, political appointment, etc.). Our IPW models by country, which are presented in Table 13, show that our findings are not driven by differences in the sample. While the magnitude of some effects may change, the cross-country order of magnitude is virtually the same.

Table 13 Average treatment effects by country using the IPW approach accounting for all covariates

	List: Shirk	**List: Sabotage**	**Vignette: Shirk**
United States	0.608*** (0.100)	0.625*** (0.113)	1.011*** (0.268)
United Kingdom	0.600*** (0.118)	0.656*** (0.120)	0.879*** (0.275)
Brazil	0.841*** (0.194)	0.970*** (0.193)	0.285 (0.553)

Note: Robust standard errors in parentheses. *** $p < 0.001$. The same covariates of Table 11 are included but omitted from the results.

6 Discussion

The most significant general finding in this research is that a substantively high proportion of civil servants say they are willing to diverge from the expected patterns of behavior for people in their positions. The literature on public servants, heavily influenced by Wilsonian tradition (Wilson 1887), emphasizes that their task is to carry out the orders of their superiors in government organizations, and to suspend their own judgments about policy and politics. We have found that civil servants are not that passive, and do have their own views about governing. Those views appear to include commitments to democratic and constitutional values. To some extent, this appears to be a return to Dwight Waldo's (1952) proposition of reconnecting democratic politics and the bureaucracy.

We should also consider the extent to which the attempts by political leaders to politicize the bureaucracy have produced a climate in which those civil servants become more politicized on their own, albeit not necessarily in the ways in which political leaders would prefer. For example, the war in Gaza has led to civil servants in foreign ministries demonstrating, *as civil servants*, against their own governments' policies (Wagemakers 2023). There may have been opposition in the past, but it is considered acceptable for civil servants to more publicly contest government policy.

At first glance, shirking and sabotage may appear to be passive or risk-averse reactions, particularly when contrasted with more direct confrontations such as public whistleblowing or formal dissent. However, this does not necessarily mean that bureaucrats who engage in these behaviors are avoiding risk altogether. On the contrary, in politicized bureaucracies – where leaders actively seek to purge noncompliant officials – withdrawing effort or subtly obstructing implementation can itself be a risky act of defiance. If these bureaucrats were truly risk-averse, they would simply comply with directives rather than taking actions – however discreet – that could jeopardize their careers.

The case of Jocelyn Samuels, a senior official at the EEOC, illustrates this dilemma: she chose open confrontation with the Trump administration and was ultimately removed from her position. While such direct challenges are crucial, they also highlight the costs of overt resistance. Many bureaucrats may choose to remain in government, engaging in less visible but still meaningful forms of opposition, ensuring that institutional resistance persists over time. The reality is that bureaucratic resistance operates on multiple levels, and subtle forms of noncompliance – though less visible – can be just as consequential in limiting the power of illiberal leaders and preserving democratic governance from within.

Those commitments to democratic values apparently are present in these three countries despite some important differences in the political systems in which they work, and in their own experiences with governments that may attempt to circumvent those democratic principles. While there are significant differences among groups of public servants in these countries, there is a general indication that they say that they would be willing to engage in these behaviors. The conventional picture of civil servants as rather risk-averse and conservative does not appear to be borne out in their expressed willingness to shirk or sabotage.

However, this willingness to resist is not uniform across all bureaucrats. The findings reveal important heterogeneities in who is more likely to engage in shirking or sabotage, suggesting that bureaucratic resistance is contingent on individual characteristics, career incentives, and institutional positioning. For instance, those who believe they could secure a well-paying job in the private sector are more willing to resist than those who perceive their career prospects outside government as weaker. This suggests that bureaucratic resistance is partly shaped by economic security – those with better outside options may feel emboldened to resist, knowing they have alternative career paths if faced with retaliation.

Additionally, the role of tenure in bureaucratic resistance appears more complex than expected. While the assumption might be that tenured bureaucrats – shielded by civil service protections – would be more resistant, our findings suggest otherwise in some cases. Untenured bureaucrats appear more willing to sabotage than tenured ones, a finding that contradicts our initial expectations. One possible explanation is that untenured officials may lack long-term investment in the institution or may be more ideologically driven, making them more willing to take risks despite their job insecurity.

Hierarchical position also plays a significant role in shaping resistance strategies. Subordinates are more likely to shirk or sabotage than their superiors, supporting the idea that bureaucratic resistance is partly a function of power asymmetries within public institutions. Those in supervisory positions may have more direct control over policy implementation, making overt resistance riskier or unnecessary, whereas subordinates – who have less direct authority – may resort to subtle, informal forms of resistance such as shirking or sabotage. Furthermore, in many cases, supervisors reached their position through a political appointment or other forms of proximity with a political patron. Given their loyalty, it becomes less likely that they will disobey their patron. This highlights that bureaucratic resistance is not just a question of ideology or democratic commitments but also a function of institutional constraints, personal risk assessments, and structural power dynamics.

Thus, while the overall findings indicate a strong willingness to resist in the face of illiberal pressures, this resistance is far from uniform. Understanding who resists, under what conditions, and through what means is crucial for scholars and policymakers seeking to anticipate bureaucratic responses to democratic backsliding. The heterogeneous responses observed in this study suggest that bureaucratic resistance is not simply a matter of personal conviction, but rather a deeply strategic, context-dependent process, influenced by job security, career mobility, and hierarchical positioning within the government.

We must also be aware that these are experimental results obtained through online, anonymous surveys. It is not clear that those civil servants who answered positively to shirking or sabotaging actually engaged in those behaviors. Answering a survey question involves no costs, while actually engaging in those behaviors may well lead to being terminated from the job, or at least reprimanded. Further, saying that one is committed to democratic values is the socially acceptable response in these societies. We must be careful in making too strong inferences from these data, but at the same time the consistency of answers across systems does lend some credence to the idea that civil servants are indeed committed to liberal democracy, and willing to act on those commitments.

6.1 Questions for Further Research

Our research has been comparative, but there is a good deal more research that should be done across time and place. One question that will need to be addressed in further research is the extent to which these findings are a function of experience with governments with illiberal tendencies. While we are arguing that Boris Johnson did not meet the usual criteria associated with a populist leader, he still was more like that type of politician than had been previous British prime ministers (Alexandre-Collier 2022; Lacatus and Meibauer 2022). Therefore, all the public servants in these samples have had some experience with leaders who appear to threaten fundamental liberal values in democracy. Do civil servants working is less obviously illiberal political systems have the same willingness to go against the wishes of an elected government?

Civil servants who have not had that experience may not be as sensitized to the threats, and therefore may be less able to conceive of themselves shirking or sabotaging in their workplace. There is evidence, for example, that prior experiences with governments in which the rule of law has been threatened does influence the behavior of officials (Kyriacou and Trivin 2024). One next step in this type of research is to conduct similar studies in societies in which populism is not a prominent part of the political environment, and to determine if there are similar results.

In a similar vein, it will be interesting to see if civil servants become less willing to engage in shirking and sabotage after the end of an illiberal regime. There have been at least three instances – Brazil, Poland and the United States – in which an illiberal regime has been replaced by elections. Has the experience of illiberal government with its threats to democratic principles altered the ways in which civil servants think about their jobs in a fundamental manner, or is the expressed willingness to engage in those nonconventional behaviors for civil servants situational and dependent upon the nature of the political regime in place at any one time?

It also appears from anecdotal evidence that the experiences of civil servants in illiberal governments have sensitized civil servants in other systems to the potential dangers of this type of behavior within government. Another potentially fruitful line of research is to investigate the extent to which there has been a general transformation of thinking about their roles among civil servants in democratic political systems. While the cases of illiberal governments have been the clearest, the general tendency to increase the politicization of the civil service may be evoking a reaction among public servants who want to defend their autonomy.

Further studies should also attempt to improve data quality, more specifically, the statistical representation of the populations they are targeting. Although they yield statistical power, our samples in Brazil are considerably small, and the convenience samples of public employees from the United States and the United Kingdom come from a large variety of organizations. Since we fielded our first survey in Brazil (see Guedes-Neto and Peters 2021), it has been replicated by Lobo (2022) and Pereira (2023) with large samples of Brazilian federal employees, respectively, public prosecutors at the National Treasury and civil servants at the Securities and Exchange Commission. In both cases, the results were fairly similar to ours. Bersch and Lotta (2023) conducted interviews with federal employees at environmental agencies to find similar evidence of willingness to resist. Future studies should consider other agencies and larger sample sizes to confirm ours and these results, as well as to map cross-agency variation in resistance to illiberal policies.

In addition to the previously stated questions, we do not know a great deal about why these civil servants are willing to express intent to depart from the usual expectations of their positions. We have made some inferences about the factors that influence that expression of commitments, based on their positions within organizations and the permanence of their appointments, but we do not have direct evidence about the justifications for their opinions, and the understandings of the civil service that are reflected in their choices. Any number of factors may be associated with the expressed willingness to deviate from the usual expectations of behavior for members of the civil service.

Furthermore, the evidence used in these studies is all about expressed willingness to engage in certain types of behaviors, rather than about actually engaging in those behaviors. The old adage that "talk is cheap" can easily be applied here. It will take a good deal of courage and commitment for a civil servant to risk his or her career over principles, even ones as important as those that may be threatened by contemporary illiberal governments. When faced with the need to decide whether to carry through with these behaviors, what would they really do?

The evidence that is readily available about the decisions of civil servants is that a significant number have been willing to leave government when faced with political leadership they find unpalatable (Ali 2019; Bolton, Figueiredo, and Lewis 2020; Dahlström and Holmgren 2019; Guedes-Neto 2022; Schuster et al. 2021). This "exit" behavior appears most obvious in the United States, but has also occurred in other governments with illiberal leaders (Barkat et al. 2024). Exit may be in some ways an easier option, especially for individuals in the upper levels of government who may be able to find new positions in think tanks or consulting rather easily. Remaining in office and attempting to undermine a government that has legitimacy from an election may be a more difficult course to follow.

This Element also focuses on the role of individual civil servants in opposing what they perceive to be illiberal or unconstitutional governments. To some extent, the decision to oppose the government and to take actions that are unconventional for public servants will be individual. However, there may be organizational and institutional factors that influence these decisions. For example, civil service systems may be more or less institutionalized in different political systems, and more institutionalized systems are likely to present less opposition to the policy demands of the government of the day. Also, some policy areas, and the organizations associated with them, may be more in the line of fire of a populist government than are others, and therefore may produce greater opposition, perhaps in order to survive,

Finally, we do not know what citizens would think of civil servants who choose to oppose the directives of their superiors in government, claiming that those orders were contrary to the constitution or to other laws. Some survey evidence, at least in the United States, reveals that citizens often trust civil servants more than they trust politicians, and therefore those citizens might be willing to accept a civil service that did resist pressures from their superiors in organizations (Hitlin and Shutava 2022; Partnership for Public Service 2022). Therefore, what may appear to some observers – perhaps especially the political leaders – as a usurpation of power, may be perceived as an appropriate response by the public servants, and as a means of supporting constitutional values.

6.2 Conclusion

This brief volume has addressed one of the most important issues of contemporary governance: how can civil servants committed to liberal democratic values work with elected governments that may not share those values? A closely linked question is how does the idea of an impartial, Weberian civil servant affect behaviors of those civil servants when fundamental constitutional and political values are being threatened. These have been, are, and will be, real questions in many democratic political systems.

The answers to the previously stated questions, when given by the civil servants themselves, are far from uniform or clear. Their behavior can be read in several ways. Several civil servants in the United States, Brazil and in other countries with illiberal leaders have chosen to leave office, but the vast majority have remained working for a government with which they may or may not agree. The evidence is that many have thought about leaving, but have chosen to stay, whether out of loyalty to the country or from personal desires to have a good career.

The answers to our questions in the survey experiment are also somewhat ambiguous. On the one hand, there were many more individuals willing to say they would shirk or sabotage than we might have expected, given the stereotypical conceptions of bureaucrats. On the other hand, there were also large numbers of civil servants who were willing to continue serving political leaders who had illiberal approaches to policy and governance. Those expressions of opinions might make advocates of the traditional civil service bargain happy, but they raise questions about the extent to which the civil service can be a bulwark against populist and illiberal values in government.

Our findings contribute to the growing literature on bureaucratic resistance, democratic backsliding, and the evolving nature of civil service neutrality.

Traditional public administration theories, particularly Weberian bureaucracy, emphasize the neutrality and professionalism of civil servants, suggesting that their primary role is to implement policy directives impartially, regardless of their personal views (Weber 1947, 1978). We already know that the separation between politics and administration did not produce that neutrality but, instead, insulated the bureaucracy to engage in its own politics (Peters 2018). Our study further explores this more complex reality, where civil servants do not always act as passive implementers but instead navigate political pressures strategically, sometimes through acts of resistance.

Brehm and Gates' (1999) triad *working*, *shirking*, and *sabotage* motivated our theoretical and methodological approach. However, while evidence so far showed that bureaucrats most often prefer to work (Pierre and Peters 2017), we demonstrate that democratic backsliding serves as a motivational trigger to turn shirking and sabotage into normatively desirable actions. This aligns with recent work on bureaucratic autonomy and resilience, which argues that civil servants are not merely reactive agents but can actively shape policy outcomes (Bersch and Fukuyama 2023; Carpenter 2002; Yesilkagit and van Thiel 2008).

Additionally, our findings contribute to scholarship on democratic erosion and state capacity, particularly the debate on whether bureaucracies function as bulwarks against illiberalism or become co-opted by political leadership (Bauer et al. 2021; Bersch and Lotta 2023; Yesilkagit et al. 2024). Building upon this literature, our findings show that resistance is conditional on economic security, hierarchical position, and tenure status, reinforcing recent arguments that bureaucrats resist selectively, based on both institutional constraints and personal risk calculations. This adds nuance to principal-agent models, which traditionally focus on mechanisms of bureaucratic control but often overlook how bureaucrats assess and manage risk in politicized environments (see, e.g., Gailmard and Patty 2007).

Moreover, our research speaks to the literature on bureaucratic exit, voice, and loyalty, particularly in contexts of political instability (Guedes-Neto 2022; Hirschman 1970; John 2017). While some scholars argue that bureaucrats facing political interference must choose between loyalty (compliance), exit (resignation), or voice (active dissent), our findings suggest that shirking and sabotage represent a mix of active and passive dissent. These behaviors allow civil servants to remain in the system while still undermining illiberal policies, supporting recent arguments that bureaucratic resistance often takes indirect, covert forms rather than open confrontation.

By integrating insights from public administration, political science, and democratic theory, this study provides a more nuanced understanding of how bureaucrats navigate illiberal governance. Rather than viewing resistance as a binary choice between compliance and confrontation, our findings suggest that bureaucratic resistance is contingent, strategic, and shaped by both institutional structures and individual incentives. Future research should further explore the conditions under which bureaucratic resistance is successful or suppressed, as well as the long-term effects of bureaucratic noncompliance on democratic stability and governance capacity.

As global challenges to democratic norms intensify, the evolving relationship between civil servants and their political environments demands closer scrutiny. The willingness of some public servants to defy conventional expectations and resist illiberal policies underscores the importance of understanding the institutional and cultural factors that influence these decisions. Future research should delve into the mechanisms that enable civil servants to either resist or comply with illiberal pressures and the long-term implications of these choices for democratic governance. As the boundaries between administrative neutrality and political engagement continue to blur, the role of civil servants in upholding constitutional principles will remain a pivotal issue for both scholars and practitioners.

In sum, the ability of civil servants to defend democratic values will depend not only on individual commitment but also on the institutional frameworks that either support or undermine their autonomy. The questions raised by this study, though complex, are essential for understanding the future of democratic governance and the role that civil servants will play in preserving or challenging the norms that define it.

References

Aberbach, Joel D., and Bert A. Rockman. 1995. "The Political Views of U.S. Senior Federal Executives, 1970–1992." *Journal of Politics* 57(3): 838–52.

Aberbach, Joel D., Robert D. Putnam, and Bert A. Rockman. 1981. *Bureaucrats and Politicians in Western Democracies*. Cambridge, USA: Harvard University Press.

Abers, Rebecca Neaera. 2019. "Bureaucratic Activism: Pursuing Environmentalism Inside the Brazilian State." *Latin American Politics and Society* 61(2): 21–44. https://doi.org/10.1017/lap.2018.75.

Abers, Rebecca Neaera, and Luciana Tatagiba. 2015. "Institutional Activism: Mobilizing for Women's Health from Inside the Brazilian Bureaucracy." In *Social Movement Dynamics*, ed. Federico M. Rossi and Marisa von Bülow. New York: Routledge, 73–102.

Alexandre-Collier, Agnès. 2022. "David Cameron, Boris Johnson and the 'Populist Hypothesis' in the British Conservative Party." *Comparative European Politics* 20(5): 527–43. https://doi.org/10.1057/s41295-022-00294-5.

Ali, Susannah Bruns. 2019. "Politics, Bureaucracy, and Employee Retention: Toward an Integrated Framework of Turnover Intent." *Administration & Society* 51(9): 1486–516. https://doi.org/10.1177/0095399718760589.

Anckar, C. 2020. "The Most Similar and Most Different Systems Design in Comparative Policy Analysis." In *Handbook of Research Methods and Applications in Comparative Policy Analysis* ed. B. G. Peters and G. Fontaine, 33–48. Cheltenham: Edward Elgar.

Auer, Matthew R. 2008. "Presidential Environmental Appointees in Comparative Perspective." *Public Administration Review* 68(1): 68–80. https://doi.org/10.1111/j.1540-6210.2007.00838.x.

Bach, Tobias, and Kai Wegrich. 2020. "Politicians and Bureaucrats in Executive Government." In *The Oxford Handbook of Political Executives*, ed. Rudy B. Andeweg, Robert Elgie, Ludger Helms, Juliet Kaarbo, and Ferdinand Müller-Rommel. Oxford: Oxford University Press, 524–46. https://academic.oup.com/edited-volume/28273/chapter-abstract/213443412?redirectedFrom=fulltext (June 27, 2023).

Baier, Vicki E., James G. March, and Harald Saetren. 1986. "Implementation and Ambiguity." *Scandinavian Journal of Management Studies* 2(3–4): 197–212.

References

Barkat, Saar, Sharon Gilad, Nir Kosti, and Ilana Shpaizman. 2025. "Civil Servants' Divergent Perceptions of Democratic Backsliding and Intended Exit, Voice and Work." https://doi.org/10.2139/ssrn.4683729.

Bauer, Michael W., B. Guy Peters, Jon Pierre, Kutsal Yesilkagit, and Stefan Becker. 2021. *Democratic Backsliding and Public Administration: How Populists in Government Transform State Bureaucracies*. Cambridge: Cambridge University Press.

Bausell, R. Barker, and Yu-Fang Li. 2006. *Power Analysis for Experimental Research: A Practical Guide for the Biological, Medical and Social Sciences*. 1st ed. Cambridge: Cambridge University Press.

Bermeo, Nancy. 2016. "On Democratic Backsliding." *Journal of Democracy* 27(1): 5–19.

Bersch, Katherine, and Francis Fukuyama. 2023. "Defining Bureaucratic Autonomy." *Annual Review of Political Science* 26(1): 213–32. https://doi.org/10.1146/annurev-polisci-051921-102914.

Bersch, Katherine, and Gabriela Lotta. 2023. "Political Control and Bureaucratic Resistance: The Case of Environmental Agencies in Brazil." *Latin American Politics and Society* 66(1): 1–24. https://doi.org/10.1017/lap.2023.22.

Bertelli, Anthony M. 2021. *Democracy Administered: How Public Administration Shapes Representative Government*. Cambridge: Cambridge University Press.

Blair, Graeme, Alexander Coppock, and Margaret Moor. 2020. "When to Worry about Sensitivity Bias: A Social Reference Theory and Evidence from 30 Years of List Experiments." *American Political Science Review* 114(4): 1297–315. https://doi.org/10.1017/S0003055420000374.

Bolton, Alexander, John M. Figueiredo, and David E. Lewis. 2020. "Elections, Ideology, and Turnover in the US Federal Government." *Journal of Public Administration Research and Theory* 31(2): 451–66.

Bourgault, Jacques. 2011. "Canada's Senior Public Service and the Typology of Bargains: From the Hierarchy of Senior Civil Servants to a Community of 'Controlled' Entrepreneurs." *Public Policy and Administration* 26(2): 253–75.

Bovens, Mark, Robert E. Goodin, and Thomas Schillemans. 2014. *The Oxford Handbook Public Accountability*. Oxford: Oxford University Press.

Bozeman, Barry, John P. Nelson, Stuart Bretschneider, and Spencer Lindsay. 2024. "The Deformation of Democracy in the United States: When Does Bureaucratic 'Neutral Competence' Rise to Complicity?" *Public Administration Review* 84(5): 796–816. https://doi.org/10.1111/puar.13855.

Brehm, John O., and Scott Gates. 1999. *Working, Shirking, and Sabotage: Bureaucratic Response to a Democratic Public*. Ann Arbor: University of Michigan Press.

References

Brierley, Sarah. 2020. "Unprincipled Principals: Co-opted Bureaucrats and Corruption in Ghana." *American Journal of Political Science* 64(2): 209–22. https://doi.org/10.1111/ajps.12495.

Carpenter, Daniel. 2002. *The Forging of Bureaucratic Autonomy: Reputations, Networks, and Policy Innovation in Executive Agencies, 1862–1928*. Princeton: Princeton University Press. https://doi.org/10.1515/9780691214078.

Cattaneo, Matias D. 2010. "Efficient Semiparametric Estimation of Multi-Valued Treatment Effects under Ignorability." *Journal of Econometrics* 155(2): 138–54.

Coppedge, Michael. 2024. "V-Dem Codebook V14: Varieties of Democracy (V-Dem) Project." www.v-dem.net/data/the-v-dem-dataset/country-year-v-dem-fullothers-v14/.

Cornell, Agnes, and Marcia Grimes. 2015. "Institutions as Incentives for Civic Action: Bureaucratic Structures, Civil Society, and Disruptive Protests." *The Journal of Politics* 77(3): 664–78. https://doi.org/10.1086/681058.

Cornell, Agnes, and Victor Lapuente. 2014. "Meritocratic Administration and Democratic Stability." *Democratization* 21(7): 1286–304.

Coyne, Christopher J., and Abigail R. Hall. 2018. *Tyranny Comes Home: The Domestic Fate of U.S. Militarism*. Stanford: Stanford University Press.

Dahlström, Carl, and Mikael Holmgren. 2019. "The Political Dynamics of Bureaucratic Turnover." *British Journal of Political Science* 49(3): 823–36.

Dahlström, Carl, and Victor Lapuente. 2012. "Weberian Bureaucracy and Corruption Prevention." In *Good Government*, ed. Sören Holmberg, and Bo Rothstein. Cheltenham: Edward Elgar, 150–73. www.elgaronline.com/edcollchap/edcoll/9780857934925/9780857934925.00015.xml (May 9, 2024).

Dahlström, Carl, and Victor Lapuente. 2022. "Comparative Bureaucratic Politics." *Annual Review of Political Science* 25(1): 43–63. https://doi.org/10.1146/annurev-polisci-051120-102543.

Dahlstrom, Carl, Victor Lapuente, and Jan Teorell. 2012. "The Merit of Meritocratization: Politics, Bureaucracy, and the Institutional Deterrents of Corruption." *Political Research Quarterly* 65(3): 656–68. https://doi.org/10.1177/1065912911408109.

Davies, Emily. 2025. "As Trump Wages War against the Federal Bureaucracy, Some Workers Fight Back." *Washington Post*. www.washingtonpost.com/politics/2025/02/07/trump-resistance-federal-workers/ (March 5, 2025).

Downs, Anthony. 1965. "A Theory of Bureaucracy." *American Economic Review* 55(1/2): 439–46.

Downs, Anthony. 1967. *Inside Bureaucracy*. Boston: Little Brown.

Driesen, David M. 2020. "The Unitary Executive Theory in Comparative Context." *Hasting Law Journal* 72: 1–54.

Finer, Herman. 1936. "Better Government Personnel." *Political Science Quarterly* 51(4): 569–99. https://doi.org/10.2307/2143948.

Friedrich, Carl J. 1935. "Responsible Government Services under the American Constitution." In *Problems of the American Public Service*, ed. Carl J. Friedrich, William C. Beyer, Sterling D. Spero, John F. Miller, and George A. Graham. New York: McGraw-Hill, 3–326.

Fukuyama, Francis. 2024. "In Defense of the Deep State." *Asia Pacific Journal of Public Administration* 46(1): 1–12. https://doi.org/10.1080/23276665.2023.2249142.

Gailmard, Sean, and John Patty. 2007. "Slackers and Zealots: Civil Service, Policy Discretion, and Bureaucratic Expertise." *American Journal of Political Science* 51(4): 873–89.

Glynn, Adam N. 2013. "What Can We Learn with Statistical Truth Serum? Design and Analysis of the List Experiment." *Public Opinion Quarterly* 77 (S1): 159–72.

Gonzales-Ocantos, Ezequiel, Chad Kiewiet de Jonge, Carlos Meléndez, Javier Osorio, and David W. Nickerson. 2012. "Vote Buying and Social Desirability Bias: Experimental Evidence from Nicaragua." *American Journal of Political Science* 56(1): 202–17.

de Graaf, Gjalt. 2011. "The Loyalties of Top Public Administrators." *Journal of Public Administration Research and Theory* 21(2): 285–306. https://doi.org/10.1093/jopart/muq028.

Guedes-Neto, João V. 2022. "Bureaucratic Polarization." Doctoral Thesis. University of Pittsburgh. http://d-scholarship.pitt.edu/42502/ (May 30, 2023).

Guedes-Neto, João V. 2023. "Bureaucrats as Legislators: The Conditional Roots of Workplace Descriptive Representation." *Representation* 59(4): 725–43. https://doi.org/10.1080/00344893.2022.2111597.

Guedes-Neto, João V. 2024. "Do You Love Me? The Effects of Budget Cuts on Intrinsic Motivation during the Trump Administration." In *Public Policy in Democratic Backsliding: How Illiberal Populists Engage with the Policy Process*, ed. Michelle Morais de Sá e Silva, and Alexandre de Ávila Gomide. New York: Springer, 311–33. https://doi.org/10.1007/978-3-031-65707-8_12.

Guedes-Neto, João V., and B. Guy Peters. 2021. "Working, Shirking, and Sabotage in Times of Democratic Backsliding: An Experimental Study in Brazil." In *Democratic Backsliding and Public Administration: How Populists in Government Transform State Bureaucracies*, ed. Michael W. Bauer, Jon Pierre, Kutsal Yesilkagit, B. Guy Peters, and Stefan Becker. Cambridge: Cambridge University Press, 221–45. https://doi.org/10.1017/9781009023504.011.

Haber, Stephen. 2013. *Crony Capitalism and Economic Growth in Latin America: Theory and Evidence*. Stanford: Hoover Institution Press.

Hajnal, György, and Zsolt Boda. 2021. "Illiberal Transformation of Government Bureaucracy in a Fragile Democracy: The Case of Hungary." In *Democratic Backsliding, Populism and Public Administration*, ed. Michael W. Bauer, B. Guy Peters, Jon Pierre, Kutsal Yesilkagit, and Stefan Becker. Cambridge: Cambridge University Press, 76–99.

Hanson, Jonathan K., and Rachel Sigman. 2021. "Leviathan's Latent Dimensions: Measuring State Capacity for Comparative Political Research." *Journal of Politics* 83(4): 1495–1510.

Hanson, Stephen E., and Jeffrey S. Kopstein. 2022. "Understanding the Global Patrimonial Wave." *Perspectives on Politics* 20(1): 237–49. https://doi.org/10.1017/S1537592721001195.

Hazell, Will. 2024. "Crackdown on 'Activists' in the Civil Service." *The Telegraph*.

Heath, Joseph. 2020. *The Machinery of Government: Public Administration and the Liberal State*. Oxford: Oxford University Press.

Heidelberg, Roy L. 2020. "Ten Theses on Accountability." *Administrative Theory & Praxis* 42(1): 6–26. https://doi.org/10.1080/10841806.2018.1512340.

Hirschman, Albert O. 1970. *Exit, Voice, and Loyalty: Responses to Decline in Firms, Organizations, and States*. Cambridge, MA: Harvard University Press.

Hitlin, Paul, and Nadzeya Shutava. 2022. "Trust in Government: A Close Look at Public Perceptions of the Federal Government and Its Employees." https://ourpublicservice.org/wp-content/uploads/2022/03/Trust-in-Government.pdf.

Hollibaugh Jr., Gary E., Matthew R. Miles, and Chad B. Newswander. 2020. "Why Public Employees Rebel: Guerrilla Government in the Public Sector." *Public Administration Review* 80(1): 64–74. https://doi.org/10.1111/puar.13118.

Hood, Christopher, and Martin Lodge. 2006. *The Politics of Public Service Bargains: Reward, Competency, Loyalty – and Blame*. Oxford: Oxford University Press.

Huber, John D., and Charles R. Shipan. 2002. *Deliberate Discretion?: The Institutional Foundations of Bureaucratic Autonomy*. Cambridge: Cambridge University Press.

Hupe, Peter. 2015. *Understanding Street-Level Bureaucracy*. Bristol: Bristol University Press.

Hustedt, Thurid, and Heidi H. Salomonsen. 2014. "Ensuring Political Responsiveness: Politicization Mechanisms in Ministerial Bureaucracies." *International Review of Administrative Sciences* 80(4): 746–65.

Imai, Kosuke, and Marc Ratkovic. 2014. "Covariate Balancing Propensity Score." *Journal of the Royal Statistical Society: Series B (Statistical Methodology)* 76(1): 243–63.

John, Peter. 2017. "Finding Exits and Voices: Albert Hirschman's Contribution to the Study of Public Services." *International Public Management Journal* 20(3): 512–29.

Khan, Naqib Ullah, Peng Zhongyi, Wajid Alim, Heesup Han, and Antonio Ariza-Montes. 2024. "Examining the Dynamics of Pro-Social Rule-Breaking among Grassroots Public Servants." *Humanities and Social Sciences Communications* 11(1): 1–13. https://doi.org/10.1057/s41599-024-03305-w.

Kuklinski, James H., Michael D. Cobb, and Martin Gilens. 1997. "Racial Attitudes and the 'New South'." *Journal of Politics* 59(2): 323–49.

Kyriacou, Andreas, and Pedro Trivin. 2024. "Populism and the Rule of Law: The Importance of Institutional Legacies." https://mpra.ub.uni-muenchen.de/120343/ (June 18, 2024).

Lacatus, Corina, and Gustav Meibauer. 2022. "'Saying It like It Is': Right-Wing Populism, International Politics, and the Performance of Authenticity." *The British Journal of Politics and International Relations* 24(3): 437–57. https://doi.org/10.1177/13691481221089137.

Liou, Kuo-Tsai, and Ronald C. Nyhan. 1994. "Dimensions of Organizational Commitment in the Public Sector: An Empirical Assessment." *Public Administration Quarterly* 18(1): 99–118.

Llorens, Jared J., and Edmund C. Stazyk. 2011. "How Important Are Competitive Wages? Exploring the Impact of Relative Wage Rates on Employee Turnover in State Government." *Review of Public Personnel Administration* 31(2): 111–27. https://doi.org/10.1177/0734371X10386184.

Lobo, José R. 2022. "A Resistência Da Burocracia Brasileira Diante de Recuos Democráticos: Uma Análise Da PGFN." Master's thesis. Fundação Getúlio Vargas.

Lodge, Martin. 2010. "Public Service Bargains in British Central Government: Multiplication, Diversification and Reassertion?" In *Tradition and Public Administration*, ed. Martin Painter, and B. Guy Peters. London: Palgrave Macmillan, 99–113. https://doi.org/10.1057/9780230289635_8.

Lotta, Gabriela, Gustavo M. Tavares, and Joana Story. 2024. "Political Attacks and the Undermining of the Bureaucracy: The Impact on Civil Servants' Well-Being." *Governance* 37(2): 619–641. https://doi.org/10.1111/gove.12792.

Lotta, Gabriela, Thomann, Michelle Fernandez, Jan Vogler, Arthur Leandro, and Marcela G. Corrêa. 2024. "Populist Government Support and Frontline Workers' Self-Efficacy during Crisis." *Governance* 37(S1): 101–25.

Lynn, Laurence E., and Robbie Waters Robichau. 2013. "Governance and Organisational Effectiveness: Towards a Theory of Government Performance." *Journal of Public Policy* 33(2): 201–28. https://doi.org/10.1017/S0143814X13000056.

Marsteintredet, Leiv, and Andrés Malamud. 2020. "Coup with Adjectives: Conceptual Stretching or Innovation in Comparative Research?" *Political Studies* 68(4): 1014–35. https://doi.org/10.1177/0032321719888857.

Mendez, Nathalie, and Claudia N. Avellaneda. 2023. "Organizational Commitment in Public Servants through Civic Engagement." *Public Administration* 101(3): 1055–71. https://doi.org/10.1111/padm.12840.

Meyer-Sahling, Jan-Hinrik, Kim Sass Mikkelsen, and Christian Schuster. 2018. "Civil Service Management and Corruption: What We Know and What We Don't." *Public Administration* 96(2): 276–85. https://doi.org/10.1111/padm.12404.

Milhorance, Carolina. 2022. "Policy Dismantling and Democratic Regression in Brazil under Bolsonaro: Coalition Politics, Ideas, and Underlying Discourses." *Review of Policy Research* 39(6): 752–70. https://doi.org/10.1111/ropr.12502.

Milhorance, Carolina, Marina Lazarotto de Andrade, Jean-François le Coq, and Eric Sabourin. 2024. "Democratic Public Action during Times of Backsliding: Examining the Resilience of Brazil's Food and Water Policies." In *Public Policy in Democratic Backsliding: How Illiberal Populists Engage with the Policy Process*, ed. Michelle Morais de Sá e Silva, and Alexandre de Ávila Gomide. Cham: Springer Nature, 227–58. https://doi.org/10.1007/978-3-031-65707-8_9.

Miller, Judith Droitcour. 1984. "A New Survey Technique for Studying Deviant Behavior." Doctoral Dissertation. George Washington University. www.proquest.com/openview/2254c7ccdade4a691e417bd5734aa874/1?pq-origsite=gscholar&cbl=18750&diss=y (February 28, 2025).

Morelli, Massimo, and Greg Sasso. 2020. "Bureaucrats under Populism." https://papers.ssrn.com/sol3/papers.cfm?abstract_id=3560307 (February 28, 2024).

Moynihan, Donald P. 2022. "Public Management for Populists: Trump's Schedule F Executive Order and the Future of the Civil Service." *Public Administration Review* 82(1): 174–78. https://doi.org/10.1111/puar.13433.

Moynihan, Donald P., and Alasdair Roberts. 2021. "Dysfunction by Design: Trumpism as Administrative Doctrine." *Public Administration Review* 81(1): 152–56.

Muno, Wolfgang, and Hector Briceño. 2021. "Venezuela: Sidelining Public Administration under a Revolutionary-Populist Regime." In *Democratic Backsliding and Public Administration: How Populists in Government*

Transform State Bureaucracies, ed. Michael W. Bauer, B. Guy Peters, Jon Pierre, Kutsal Yesilkagit, and Stefan Becker. Cambridge: Cambridge University Press, 200–220.

Mutz, Diana Carole. 2011. *Population-Based Survey Experiments*. Princeton: Princeton University Press.

Nabatchi, Tina, and Lisa Blomgren Amsler. 2014. "Direct Public Engagement in Local Government." *The American Review of Public Administration* 44-(4_suppl): 63S–88S. https://doi.org/10.1177/0275074013519702.

Neuhold, Christine. 2014. *More Bureaucracy or More Democracy: The EU at an "Unrepresentative Turn"?* Maastricht: Maastricth University.

Newhouse, Sean Michael. 2025. "2 Equal Employment Opportunity Commission Democrats Fired." *Government Executive*. www.govexec.com/transition/2025/01/two-equal-employment-opportunity-commission-democrats-fired/402568/ (March 5, 2025).

Nieto-Morales, Fernando, Rik Peeters, and Gabriela Lotta. 2024. "Burdens, Bribes, and Bureaucrats: The Political Economy of Petty Corruption and Administrative Burdens." *Journal of Public Administration Research and Theory* 34(4): 481–97. https://doi.org/10.1093/jopart/muae010.

O'Donnell, Guillermo. 1994. "Delegative Democracy." *Journal of Democracy* 5(1): 55–69.

O'Leary, Rosemary. 2019. *The Ethics of Dissent: Managing Guerrilla Government*. Washington D.C.: CQ Press.

Oliveros, Virginia. 2016. "Making It Personal: Clientelism, Favors, and the Personalization of Public Administration in Argentina." *Comparative Politics* 48(3): 373–91.

Olsen, Johan P. 2017. *Democratic Accountability, Political Order, and Change: Exploring Accountability Processes in an Era of European Transformation*. Oxford: Oxford University Press.

Olsson, Jan. 2016. *Subversion in Institutional Change and Stability: A Neglected Mechanism*. New York: Springer.

Ozymy, Joshua, Bryan Menard, and Melissa L. Jarrell. 2021. "Persistence or Partisanship: Exploring the Relationship between Presidential Administrations and Criminal Enforcement by the US Environmental Protection Agency, 1983–2019." *Public Administration Review* 81(1): 49–63. https://doi.org/10.1111/puar.13295.

Panizza, Francisco, B. Guy Peters, and Conrado Ramos Larraburu. 2023. *The Politics of Patronage Appointments in Latin American Central Administrations*. Pittsburgh: University of Pittsburgh Press.

Partnership for Public Service. 2022. "Trust in Government." https://ourpublicservice.org/publications/trust-in-government/.

Pereira, Marcelo M. 2023. "Burocracia Sob Ataque: (Re)Ações Diante de Retrocessos Democráticos." Dissertação de Mestrado. Fundação Getúlio Vargas.

Perry, James L. 1997. "Antecedents of Public Service Motivation." *Journal of Public Administration Research and Theory* 7(2): 181–97.

Perry, James L. 2000. "Bringing Society In: Toward a Theory of Public-Service Motivation." *Journal of Public Administration Research and Theory* 10(2): 471–88. https://doi.org/10.1093/oxfordjournals.jpart.a024277.

Perry, James L., and Lois Recascino Wise. 1990. "The Motivational Bases of Public Service." *Public Administration Review* 50(3): 367–73.

Perugini, Marco, Marcello Gallucci, and Giulio Costantini. 2018. "A Practical Primer to Power Analysis for Simple Experimental Designs." *International Review of Social Psychology* 31(1): 1–23. https://doi.org/10.5334/irsp.181.

Peters, B. Guy. 1987. "Bureaucrats and Politicians." In *Bureaucracy and Public Choice*, ed. Jan-Erik Lane. London: Sage.

Peters, B. Guy. 2018. *The Politics of Bureaucracy: An Introduction to Comparative Public Administration.* 7th ed. New York: Routledge.

Peters, B. Guy. 2021. *Administrative Traditions: Understanding the Roots of Contemporary Administrative Behavior.* Oxford: Oxford University Press.

Peters, B. Guy, and Donald J. Savoie. 1994. "Civil Service Reform: Misdiagnosing the Patient." *Public Administration Review* 54: 418–25.

Peters, B. Guy, and João V. Guedes-Neto. 2020. "Experimental Methods A: Survey Experiments in Public Administration." In *Handbook of Research Methods in Public Administration, Management and Policy*, ed. Eran Vigoda-Gadot, and Dana R. Vashdi. Cheltenham: Edward Elgar, 218–33.

Peters, B. Guy, and Jon Pierre. 2000. "Citizens versus the New Public Manager: The Problem of Mutual Empowerment." *Administration & Society* 32(1): 9–28.

Peters, B. Guy, and Jon Pierre. 2004. *Politicization of the Civil Service in Comparative Perspective: The Quest for Control.* New York: Routledge.

Peters, B. Guy, and Jon Pierre. 2019. "Populism and Public Administration: Confronting the Administrative State." *Administration & Society* 51(10): 1521–45. https://doi.org/10.1177/0095399719874749.

Peters, B. Guy, and Jon Pierre. 2022. "Politicisation of the Public Service during Democratic Backsliding: Alternative Perspectives." *Australian Journal of Public Administration* 81: 629–39.

Phillips, Tom. 2018. "Trump of the Tropics: The 'dangerous' Candidate Leading Brazil's Presidential Race." *The Guardian.* www.theguardian.com/world/2018/apr/19/jair-bolsonaro-brazil-presidential-candidate-trump-paralels (March 5, 2025).

Pierre, Jon, and B. Guy Peters. 2017. "The Shirking Bureaucrat: A Theory in Search of Evidence?" *Policy & Politics* 45(2): 157–72.

Przeworski, Adam, and Henry Teune. 1982. *The Logic of Comparative Social Inquiry*. Malabar: Krieger.

Rawnsley, Andrew. 2020. "The Civil Service Is Right to Be Paranoid about Boris Johnson's Gang of Three." *The Guardian*. www.theguardian.com/commentisfree/2020/jul/05/the-civil-service-is-right-to-be-paranoid-about-boris-johnsons-gang-of-three (February 11, 2025).

Rich, Jessica. 2013. "Grassroots Bureaucracy: Intergovernmental Relations and Popular Mobilization in Brazil's AIDS Policy Sector." *Latin American Perspectives* 55(2): 1–25.

Ringquist, Evan J. 1995. "Political Control and Policy Impact in EPA's Office of Water Quality." *American Journal of Political Science* 39(2): 336–63. https://doi.org/10.2307/2111616.

Sá e Silva, Michelle. 2020. "Once Upon a Time, a Human Rights Ally: The State and Its Bureaucracy in Right-Wing Populist Brazil." *Human Rights Quarterly* 42(3): 646–66. https://doi.org/10.1353/hrq.2020.0036.

Sá e Silva, Michelle. 2022. "Policy Dismantling by Capacity Manipulation in a Context of Democratic Backsliding: The Bureaucracy in Disarray in Bolsonaro's Brazil." *International Review of Public Policy* 4(3): 272–92.

Sager, Fritz, and Christian Rosser. 2009. "Weber, Wilson, and Hegel: Theories of Modern Bureaucracy." *Public Administration Review* 69(6): 1136–47. https://doi.org/10.1111/j.1540-6210.2009.02071.x.

Schmitter, Philippe C. 1971. *Interest Conflict and Political Change in Brazil*. Stanford: Stanford University Press.

Schuster, Christian, Jan-Hinrik Meyer-Sahling, and Kim Sass Mikkelsen. 2020. "(Un)Principled Principals, (Un)Principled Agents: The Differential Effects of Managerial Civil Service Reforms on Corruption in Developing and OECD Countries." *Governance* 33(4): 829–48.

Schuster, Christian, Kim Sass Mikkelsen, Izabela Correa, and Jan-Hinrik Meyer-Sahling. 2021. "Exit, Voice, and Sabotage: Public Service Motivation and Guerrilla Bureaucracy in Times of Unprincipled Political Principals." *Journal of Public Administration Research and Theory* 32(2): 416–35. https://doi.org/10.1093/jopart/muab028.

Selden, Sally Coleman, and Donald P. Moynihan. 2000. "A Model of Voluntary Turnover in State Government." *Review of Public Personnel Administration* 20(2): 63–74. https://doi.org/10.1177/0734371X0002000206.

Silveira, Mariana Costa, Nissim Cohen, and Gabriela Lotta. 2024. "Are Bureaucrats' Interactions with Politicians Linked to the Bureaucrats' Policy

Entrepreneurship Tendencies?" *Policy Studies Journal* 52(3): 533–59. https://doi.org/10.1111/psj.12536.

Sniderman, Paul M., James N. Druckman, Donald P. Green, James H. Kuklinski, and Arthur Lupia. 2011. "The Logic and Design of the Survey Experiment." In *Cambridge Handbook of Experimental Political Science*, ed. James N. Druckman, Donald P. Greene, and James H. Kuklinski . Cambridge: Cambridge University Press, 102–14.

Staranova, Katarina, and Colin Knox. 2024. "Dimensions of Politicization." In *Handbook of Political Patronage and Politicization*, ed. B. Guy Peters, Colin Knox, Francisco Panizza, Conrado Ramos Larraburu, and Katarina Staranova. Cheltenham: Edward Elgar, 15–40.

Story, Joana, Gabriela Lotta, and Gustavo M. Tavares. 2023. "(Mis)Led by an Outsider: Abusive Supervision, Disengagement, and Silence in Politicized Bureaucracies." *Journal of Public Administration Research and Theory* 33(4): 549–62. muad004. https://doi.org/10.1093/jopart/muad004.

Suzuki, Kohei, and Hyunkang Hur. 2020. "Bureaucratic Structures and Organizational Commitment: Findings from a Comparative Study of 20 European Countries." *Public Management Review* 22: 877–907.

Trippenbach, Ivanne. 2024. "Face á Un Possible Gouvernement d'extrême Droi, Les Cadres de l'Etat 'Tétanisês'." *Le Monde*. www.lemonde.fr/politique/article/2024/06/15/face-a-un-possible-gouvernement-d-extreme-droite-la-tetanie-des-cadres-de-l-etat_6240170_823448.html.

Tullock, Gordon. 2005. "The Politics of Bureaucracy: Bureaucracy (1965)." In *Selected Works of Gordon Tullock*, ed. C. K. Rowley. Indianapolis: Liberty Fund, 1–238.

Tullock, Gordon, Arthur Seldon, and Gordon L. Brady. 2002. *Government Failure: A Primer on Public Choice*. Washington, DC: Cato Institute.

V-Dem Institute. 2020. "Democracy Facing Global Challenges: V-Dem Annual Democracy Report 2019."

Wagemakers, Tim. 2023. "De Activistische Ambtenaar Is in Opkomst: Loyaal Aan Bestuur of Aan Eigen Moraal?" *Het Parool*. www.parool.nl/politiek/de-activistische-ambtenaar-is-in-opkomst-loyaal-aan-bestuur-of-aan-eigen-moraal~b7788fbf/.

Wagner, Erich. 2025. "New Schedule F Guidance Shows the Trump White House Is Rearing for a Fight." *Government Executive*. www.govexec.com/workforce/2025/01/new-schedule-f-guidance-shows-trump-white-house-rearing-fight/402532/ (March 5, 2025).

Waisbich, Laura T. 2024. "Mobilising International Embeddedness to Resist Radical Policy Change and Dismantling: The Case of Brazil under Jair Bolsonaro (2019–2022)." *Policy Sciences* 57(3): 1–25.

Waldo, Dwight. 1948. *The Administrative State: A Study of the Political Theory of American Public Administration*. New York: The Ronald Press.

Waldo, Dwight. 1952. "Development of Theory of Democratic Administration." *American Political Science Review* 46(1): 81–103. https://doi.org/10.2307/1950764.

Weber, Max. 1947. *The Theory of Social and Economic Organizations*. New York: Free Press.

Weber, Max. 1978. *Economy and Society: An Outline of Interpretive Sociology*, ed. Guenther Roth, and Claus Wittich. Berkeley: University of California Press.

Wilson, Woodrow. 1887. "The Study of Administration." *Political Science Quarterly* 2(2): 197–222.

Withey, Michael J., and William H. Cooper. 1989. "Predicting Exit, Voice, Loyalty, and Neglect." *Administrative Science Quarterly* 34(4): 521–39. https://doi.org/10.2307/2393565.

Yesilkagit, Kutsal, Michael W. Bauer, B. Guy Peters, and Jon Pierre. 2024. "The Guardian State: Strengthening the Public Service against Democratic Backsliding."

Yesilkagit, Kutsal, and Sandra van Thiel. 2008. "Political Influence and Bureaucratic Autonomy." *Public Organization Review* 8(2): 137–53. https://doi.org/10.1007/s11115-008-0054-7.

Zhang, Liwei, Ji Zhao, and Weiwei Dong. 2021. "Street-Level Bureaucrats as Policy Entrepreneurs: Action Strategies for Flexible Community Governance in China." *Public Administration* 99(3): 469–83. https://doi.org/10.1111/padm.12730.

Public and Nonprofit Administration

Robert Christensen
Brigham Young University
Robert Christensen is the George W. Romney Professor of Public and Nonprofit Management at Brigham Young University.

Jaclyn Piatak
University of North Carolina at Charlotte
Jaclyn Piatak is co-editor of NVSQ and Professor of Political Science and Public Administration at the University of North Carolina at Charlotte.

Rosemary O'Leary
University of Kansas
Rosemary O'Leary is the Edwin O. Stene Distinguished Professor Emerita of Public Administration at the University of Kansas.

About the Series
The foundation of this series are cutting-edge contributions on emerging topics and definitive reviews of keystone topics in public and nonprofit administration, especially those that lack longer treatment in textbook or other formats. Among keystone topics of interest for scholars and practitioners of public and nonprofit administration, it covers public management, public budgeting and finance, nonprofit studies, and the interstitial space between the public and nonprofit sectors, along with theoretical and methodological contributions, including quantitative, qualitative and mixed-methods pieces.

The Public Management Research Association
The Public Management Research Association improves public governance by advancing research on public organizations, strengthening links among interdisciplinary scholars, and furthering professional and academic opportunities in public management.

Cambridge Elements

Public and Nonprofit Administration

Elements in the Series

Public Administration and Democracy: The Complementarity Principle
Anthony M. Bertelli and Lindsey J. Schwartz

Redefining Development: Resolving Complex Challenges in a Global Context 2nd edition
Jessica Kritz

Experts in Government: The Deep State from Caligula to Trump and Beyond
Donald F. Kettl

New Public Governance as a Hybrid: A Critical Interpretation
Laura Cataldi

Can Governance be Intelligent?: An Interdisciplinary Approach and Evolutionary Modelling for Intelligent Governance in the Digital Age
Eran Vigoda-Gadot

The Courts and the President: Judicial Review of Presidentially Directed Action
Charles Wise

Standing Up for Nonprofits: Advocacy on Federal, Sector-wide Issues
Alan J. Abramson and Benjamin Soskis

Topics in Public Administration: Perspectives from Computational Social Sciences and Corpus Linguistics
Richard M. Walker, Jiasheng Zhang and Yanto Chandra

Public Service Explained: The Role of Citizens in Value Creation
Greta Nasi, Stephen Osborne, Maria Cucciniello and Tie Cui

Court-Ordered Community Service: The Experiences of Community Organizations and Community Service Workers
Rebecca Nesbit, Su Young Choi and Jody Clay-Warner

Sustainable Inclusion through Performance-Driven Practices: An Evidence-Based, Dynamic Systems Framework
Ruth Sessler Bernstein and Paul Salipante

Bureaucratic Resistance in Times of Democratic Backsliding
João V. Guedes-Neto and B. Guy Peters

A full series listing is available at: www.cambridge.org/EPNP

For EU product safety concerns, contact us at Calle de José Abascal, 56–1°, 28003 Madrid, Spain or eugpsr@cambridge.org.

www.ingramcontent.com/pod-product-compliance
Lightning Source LLC
LaVergne TN
LVHW011857060526
838200LV00054B/4378